The Mathematics of the
Ideal Villa and Other Essays

# The Mathematics of the
# Ideal Villa and Other Essays

Colin Rowe

The MIT Press
Cambridge, Massachusetts,
and London, England

Fourth printing, 1985
First MIT Press paperback edition, 1982
Copyright ©1976 by

The Massachusetts Institute of Technology

This book was set in IBM Composer Theme by Techdata Associates, Inc. and printed and bound by The Murray Printing Company in the United States of America.

Library of Congress Cataloging in Publication Data

Rowe, Colin.
  The mathematics of the ideal villa and other essays.

  Includes bibliographical references.
  CONTENTS: The mathematics of the ideal villa.—Mannerism and modern architecture.—Character and composition.—Chicago frame. [etc.]
  1. Architecture, Domestic—Addresses, essays, lectures. I. Title.
NA7110.R68      720'.8      75-33908
ISBN 0-262-18077-4 (hard)
      0-262-68037-8 (paper)

# Contents

Preface and Acknowledgments    vii

The Mathematics of the
Ideal Villa                    1

Mannerism and Modern
Architecture                   29

Character and Composition;
or Some Vicissitudes of
Architectural Vocabulary
in the Nineteenth Century      59

Chicago Frame                  89

Neo-'Classicism' and
Modern Architecture I          119

Neo-'Classicism' and
Modern Architecture II         139

Transparency: Literal
and Phenomenal
(with Robert Slutzky)          159

La Tourette                    185

The Architecture of
Utopia                         205

Picture Credits                225

# Preface and
# Acknowledgments

This is a collection of essays mostly written long ago, some of them published long ago and, therefore, 'old,' and some of them published only recently and, therefore, 'old-new.'

Had it not been for inertia this particular collection might well have been published in the early Sixties; but, while I sometimes regret that this was not done, I am by no means dismayed by the delay. For most of these essays have remained, in some degree, relevant and some of them have long enjoyed a piratical, xeroxed, student circulation which, to me, can only be gratifying.

However, if such is the ultimate reason for this book, then, after conceding this initiatory stimulus, I must add that it is to John Entenza, until recently Director of the Graham Foundation, that I am most particularly indebted for insisting on a definitive publication. The Graham Foundation subsidized and Mr. Entenza almost provoked; but, apart from their liberality and their demands, I would wish to acknowledge, in England, Alan Colquhoun, James Stirling, John Miller, and Patrick Hodgkinson—by all of whom I have been pressured, and, in the United States, Fred Koetter, Peter Eisenman, Arthur Drexler, and Stanford Anderson; who have, all of them, intimated that what is here published is not bizarre. Then I owe a particular debt to Robert Slutzky for many illuminations and for his willingness to allow an article of joint authorship to appear in this anthology; I am indebted to the editors of *Architectural Review, Granta, Perspecta,* and *Oppositions* for permission to publish such material as originally appeared in their pages; I wish to thank Joel Bostick for his efforts in preparing analytical diagrams of Garches, the Malcontenta, and the Palais des Nations; and, finally, I wish to express my appreciation to Judith Holliday for her heroic efforts in reading and correcting the proofs of this manuscript.

# The Mathematics of the
# Ideal Villa

First published in the *Architectural Review*,
1947.

There are two causes of beauty—natural and customary. Natural is from geometry consisting in uniformity, that is equality and proportion. Customary beauty is begotten by the use, as familiarity breeds a love for things not in themselves lovely. Here lies the great occasion of errors, but always the true test is natural or geometrical beauty. Geometrical figures are naturally more beautiful than irregular ones: the square, the circle are the most beautiful, next the parallelogram and the oval. There are only two beautiful positions of straight lines, perpendicular and horizontal; this is from Nature and consequently necessity, no other than upright being firm.

—Sir Christopher Wren, Parentalia

As the ideal type of centralized building Palladio's Villa Capra-Rotonda (Plate 1) has, perhaps more than any other house, imposed itself upon the imagination. Mathematical, abstract, four square, without apparent function and totally memorable, its derivatives have enjoyed universal distribution; and, when he writes of it, Palladio is lyrical.

The site is as pleasant and delightful as can be found, because it is on a small hill of very easy access, and is watered on one side by the Bacchiglione, a navigable river; and on the other it is encompassed about with most pleasant risings which look like a very great theatre and are all cultivated about with most excellent fruits and most exquisite vines; and therefore as it enjoys from every part most beautiful views, some of which are limited, some more extended, and others which terminate with the horizon, there are loggias made in all four fronts.[1]

When the mind is prepared for the one by the other, a passage from Le Corbusier's *Précisions* may be unavoidably reminiscent of this. No less lyrical but rather more explosive, Le Corbusier is describing the site of his Savoye House at Poissy (Plate 2).

Le site: une vaste pelouse bombée en dôme aplati. . . . La maison est une boîte en l'air . . . au milieu des prairies dominant le verger. . . . Le plan est pur. . . . Il à sa juste place dans l'agreste paysage de Poissy. . . . Les habitants, venus ici parce que cette campagne agreste était belle avec *sa vie de campagne*, ils la contempleront, maintenue intacte, du haut de leur jardin suspendu ou des quatre faces de leurs fenêtres en longueur. Leur vie domestique sera inserée dans un rêve virgilien.[2]

The Savoye House has been given a number of interpretations. It may indeed be a machine for living in, an arrangement of interpenetrating volumes and spaces, an emanation of space-time; but the suggestive reference to the dreams of Virgil may put one in mind of the passage in which Palladio describes the Rotonda. Palladio's landscape is more agrarian and bucolic, he evokes less of the untamed pastoral, his scale is larger; but the effect of the two passages is somehow the same.

Palladio, writing elsewhere, amplifies the ideal life of the villa. Its owner, from within a fragment of created order, will watch the maturing of his possessions and savor the piquancy of contrast between his fields and his gardens; reflecting on mutability, he will contemplate throughout the years the antique virtues of a simpler race, and the harmonious ordering of his life and his estate will be an analogy of paradise.

**The ancient sages commonly used to retire to such places, where being oftentimes visited by their virtuous friends and relations, having houses, gardens, fountains and such like pleasant places, and above all their virtue, they could easily attain to as much happiness as can be attained here below.[3]**

Perhaps these were the dreams of Virgil; and, freely interpreted, they have gathered around themselves in the course of time all those ideas of Roman virtue, excellence, Imperial splendor, and decay which make up the imaginative reconstruction of the ancient world. It would have been, perhaps, in the landscapes of Poussin—with their portentous apparitions of the antique—that Palladio would have felt at home; and it is possibly the fundamentals of this landscape, the poignancy of contrast between the disengaged cube and its setting in the *paysage agreste*, between geometrical volume and the appearance of unimpaired nature, which lie behind Le Corbusier's Roman allusion. If architecture at the Rotonda forms the setting for the good life, at Poissy it is certainly the background for the lyrically efficient one; and, if the contemporary pastoral is not yet sanctioned by conventional usage, apparently the Virgilian nostalgia is still present. From the hygenically equipped boudoirs, pausing while ascending the ramps, the memory of the Georgics no doubt interposes itself; and, perhaps, the historical reference may even add a stimulus as the car pulls out for Paris.

However, a more specific comparison which presents itself is that between Palladio's Villa Foscari, the Malcontenta of *c.* 1550-60 (Plates 3, 4), and the house which in 1927 Le Corbusier built for Mr. and Mrs. Michael Stein at Garches (Plates 5, 6).

These are two buildings which, in their forms and evocations, are superficially so entirely unlike that to bring them together would seem to be facetious; but, if the obsessive psychological and physical gravity of the Malcontenta receives no parallel in a house which sometimes wishes to be a ship, sometimes a gymnasium, this difference of mood should not be allowed to inhibit scrutiny.

For, in the first case, both Garches and the Malcontenta are conceived of as single blocks (Plates 7, 8); and, allowing for variations in roof treatment, it might be noticed that both are blocks of corresponding volume, each measuring 8 units in length, by 5½ in breadth, by 5 in height. Then, further to this, there is a comparable bay structure to be observed. Each house exhibits (and conceals) an alternating rhythm of double and single spatial intervals; and each house, read from front to back, displays a comparable tripartite distribution of lines of support (Figure 1).

But, at this stage, it might be better to introduce an *almost*. Because, if the distribution of basic horizontal coordinates is, in both cases, much the same, there are still some slight and significant differences relating to the distribution of those lines of support which parallel the facades; and thus at Garches, reading from front to back, the fundamental spatial interval proceeds in the ratio of ½ : 1½ : 1½ : 1½ : ½, while at the Malcontenta we are presented with the sequence 2 : 2 : 1½. In other words, by the use of a cantilevered half unit Le Corbusier obtains a compression for his central bay and thereby transfers interest elsewhere; while Palladio secures a dominance for his central division with a progression towards his portico which absolutely focuses attention in these two areas. The one scheme is, therefore, potentially dispersed and possibly equalitarian and the other is concentric and certainly hierarchical; but, with this difference observed, it might simply be added that, in both cases, a projecting element—extruded terrace or attached portico—occupies 1½ units in depth.

Structures, of course, are not to be compared; and, to some extent, both architects look to structure as a justification for their dispositions. Thus Palladio employs a solid bearing wall; and of this system he writes:

It is to be observed, that those (rooms) on the right correspond with those on the left, that so the fabric may be the same in one place as in the other, and that the walls may equally bear the burden of the roof; because if the walls are made large in one part and small in the other, the latter will be more firm to resist the weight, by reason of the nearness of the walls, and the former more weak, which will produce in time very great inconveniences and ruin the whole work.[4]

Palladio is concerned with the logical disposition of motifs dogmatically accepted, but he attempts to discover a structural reason for his planning symmetries; while Le Corbusier, who is proving a case for structure as a basis for the formal elements of design, contrasts the new system with the old and is a little more comprehensive.

Je vous rappelle ce "plan paralyse" de la maison de pierre et ceci à quoi nous sommes arrivés avec la maison de fer ou de ciment armé.
    plan libre
    façade libre

Figure 1   Malcontenta and Garches. Analytical diagrams.

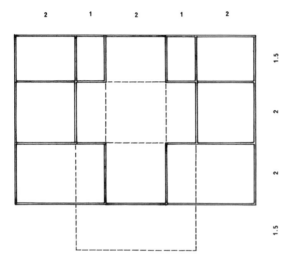

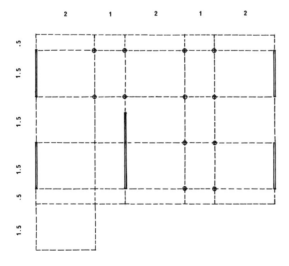

ossature indépendante
fenêtres en longueur ou pan de verre
pilotis
toit-jardin
et l'intérieur muni de "casiers" et débarrassé de l'encombrement des meubles.[5]

Palladio's structural system makes it almost necessary to repeat the same plan on every level of the building, while point support allows Le Corbusier a flexible arrangement; but both architects make a claim which is somewhat in excess of the reasons they advance. Solid wall structures, Palladio declares, demand absolute symmetry; a frame building, Le Corbusier announces, requires a free arrangement: but these must be, at least partly, the personal exigencies of high style—for asymmetrical buildings of traditional structure remain standing and even frame buildings of conventional plan continue to give satisfaction.

In both houses there is a *piano nobile* one floor up, which is linked to the garden by a terrace or portico and a flight (or flights) of steps. At the Malcontenta this main floor shows a cruciform hall with, symmetrically disposed about it, two suites of three rooms each and two staircases; but at Garches there is nothing so readily describable. At Garches there is a central hall and there are two staircases; but while one of the staircases occupies a similar position to those of the Malcontenta, the other has been turned through an angle of ninety degrees. Further, the entrance hall has been revealed from this level by an asymmetrical cutting open of the floor; and the terrace (which corresponds to the Malcontenta's portico) has become partly a reentrant volume obliterating a line of support, placed in distinctly less perceptible relationship to the principal room. Thus, at Garches, the cruciform shape survives only vestigially (perhaps it may be thought to be registered by the apse of the dining room?); and therefore, instead of the centrality of Palladio's major space, a Z-shaped balance is achieved which is assisted by throwing the small library into the main apartment. Finally, while at the Malcontenta there is a highly evident cross axis, at Garches this transverse movement which is intimated by the central voids of the end walls is only allowed to develop implicitly and by fragments.

The wall at the Malcontenta comprises the traditional solid pierced by vertical openings with a central emphasis in the portico and subsidiary accents in the outer windows placed toward the extremities of the facade. The double bay in the center of the building which carries the upper pediments of the roof is expressed on the one front by a single door, on the other by a 'Roman baths' motif; and, horizontally, the wall also falls into three primary divisions: base; *piano nobile*, corresponding to the Ionic order of the portico; and superimposed attic. The base plays the part of a projecting, consistently supporting solid upon which the house rests; but, while the *piano nobile* and attic are rusticated, the base is treated as a plain surface and a feeling of even greater weight carried here is achieved by this highly emotive inversion of the usual order.

Again the situation at Garches is more complex; and there the exploitation of the structural system has led to a conception of the wall as a series of horizontal strips—a strategy which places equal interest in both center and extremity of the facade and which is then maintained by Le Corbusier's tendency to suppress the wider spans of the double bays. By these means any system of central vertical accent and inflection of the wall leading up to it is profoundly modified; and the immediate result in the garden elevation of Garches shows itself in the displacing of the elements which may be considered equivalent to the Malcontenta's portico and superimposed pediment. These become separate; and, transposed as terrace and roof pavilion, the one occupies the two (or three) bays to the left of the facade, the other a central position in the solid but an asymmetrical one in the whole elevation.

On the other hand, the entrance front at Garches retains what could be regarded as the analogue of Palladio's upper pediment. This is the central element of the upper story; but then it is also noticeable, in spite of its symmetrical position, that the further development of this element within itself is not symmetrical. Nor does it promote symmetry in the facade as a whole; and, though it is responded to by the large central window of the entrance hall, since the horizontal gashes of the windows act to prohibit any explicit linking of these two manifestations, there ensues in the elevation something very like that simultaneous affirmation and denial of centrality which is displayed in the plan. Thus a central focus is stipulated; its development is inhibited; and there then occurs a displacement and a breaking up of exactly what Palladio would have presumed to be a normative emphasis.

Another chief point of difference lies in the interpretation of the roof. At the Malcontenta this forms a pyramidal superstructure which amplifies the volume of the house (Plate 9); while at Garches it is constituted by a flat surface, serving as the floor of an enclosure, cut out from—and thereby diminishing—the house's volume. Thus, in the one building the behavior of the roof might be described as additive and in the other as subtractive; but, this important distinction apart, both roofs are then furnished with a variety of incident, regular or random, pediment or pavilion, which alike enter into important—though very different—relationships with the vertical surfaces of the walls below.

That mathematics and musical concord were the basis of ideal proportion was a common belief of the circles in which Palladio moved. Here there was felt to be a correspondence between the perfect numbers, the proportions of the human figure and the elements of musical harmony;[6] and Sir Henry Wotton, as British ambassador to Venice at a slightly later date, reflects some part of this attitude when he writes:

**The two principal Consonances that most ravish the Ear are, by the consent of all Nature, the *Fifth* and the *Octave*; whereof the first riseth radically, from the Proportion between two and three. The other from the double Interval, between one and two, or between two and four, etc. Now if we shall transport these Proportions, from audible to visible Objects, and apply them as shall fall fittest . . . , there will indubitably result from either, a graceful and harmonious Contentment to the Eye.[7]**

It was not, in fact, suggested that architectural proportions were derived from musical harmonies, but rather that the laws of proportion were established mathematically and everywhere diffused. The universe of Platonic and Pythagorean speculation was compounded of the simpler relationships of numbers, and such a cosmos was formed within the triangle made by the square and the cube of the numbers 1, 2, 3. Also, its qualities, rhythms, and relationships were established within this framework of numbers up to 27; and if such numbers governed the works of God, it was considered fitting that the works of man should be similarly constructed, that a building should be a representative, in microcosm, of the process exhibited at a larger scale in the workings of the world. In Alberti's words: *"Nature is sure to act consistently and with a constant analogy in all her operations"*;[8] and, therefore, what is patent in music must also be so in architecture. Thus, with proportion as a projection of the harmony of the universe, its basis— both scientific and religious—was quite unassailable; and a Palladio could enjoy the satisfactions of an aesthetic believed to be entirely objective.

Le Corbusier has expressed similar convictions about proportion. Mathematics bring *"des vérités réconfortantes,"* and *"on ne quitte pas son ouvrage qu'avec la certitude d'être arrivé à la chose exacte"*;[9] but if it is indeed exactness which Le Corbusier seeks, within his buildings it is not the unchallengeable clarity of Palladio's volumes which one finds. It is, instead, a type of planned obscurity; and, consequently, while in the Malcontenta geometry is diffused throughout the internal volumes of the entire building, at Garches it seems only to reside in the block as a whole and in the disposition of its supports.

The theoretical position upon which Palladio's position rested broke down in the eighteenth century when proportion became a matter of individual sensibility and private inspiration;[10] and Le Corbusier, in spite of the comforts which mathematics afford him, simply in terms of his location in history can occupy no such unassailable position. Functionalism was, perhaps, a highly Positivistic attempt to reassert a scientific aesthetic which might possess the objective value of the old, and the ultimately Platonic-Aristotelian critique. But its interpretation was crude. Results may be measured in terms of process, proportions are apparently accidental and gratuitous; and it is in contradiction to this theory that Le Corbusier imposes mathematical patterns upon his buildings. These are the universal "*vérités réconfortantes.*"

Thus, either because of or in spite of theory both architects share a common standard, a mathematical one, defined by Wren as "natural" beauty; and, within limitations of a particular program, it should therefore not be surprising that the two blocks should be of corresponding volume or that both architects should choose to make didactic advertisement of their adherence to mathematical formulae. Of the two—and, perhaps, characteristically—Le Corbusier is the more aggressive; and at Garches he carefully indicates his relationships by an apparatus of regulating lines and figures and by placing on the drawings of his elevations the ratio of the golden section, $A : B = B : (A + B)$ (Figure 2).

But, if Le Corbusier's facades are for him the primary demonstrations of the virtues of a mathematical discipline, with Palladio it would seem that the ultimate proof of his theory lies in his plan. Throughout his *Quattro libri*, Palladio consistently equips both his plans and elevations with their numerical apologetic (Plate 8); but the cryptic little figures which he appends to his drawings seem always to be more convincing, or at least more comprehensible, when they relate to the plan. And this is, possibly, to be understood, for in a house such as the Malcontenta the plan may be seen as an exhibition of 'natural' beauty, as the pure thing, abstract and uncomplicated; but the facades are, of necessity, adulterated (though scarcely to their detriment) by an intrusion of 'customary' material. The facades become complicated, their strict Platonic rationale may be ultimately vitiated by the traditional presence, in this case, of the Ionic order which possesses its own rationale and which inevitably introduces an alternative system of measurement (Plate 11).

The conflict between the 'customary' demands of the order and a series of 'natural' relationships might be assumed to be the source from which the facades of the Malcontenta derive. They are suggestive, evocative, but they are not easily or totally susceptible to mathematical regulation; and, therefore, it is again toward Palladio's plan that one reverts. Provided with explanatory dimensions, the two

Figure 2   Garches, elevations.

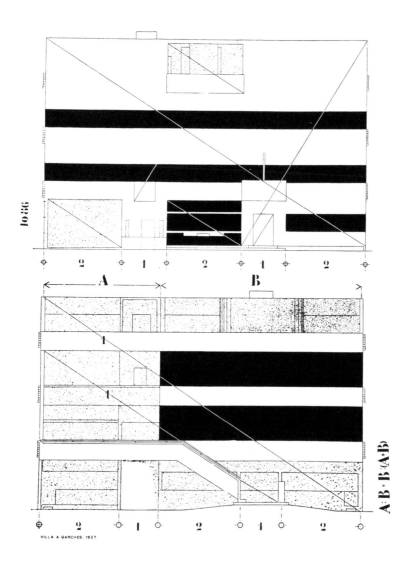

suites comprising three rooms each can be read as a progression from 3 : 4 to a 2 : 3 relationship. They are numbered 12 : 16, 16 : 16 and 16 : 24.

And here, on the part of Le Corbusier and Palladio, we have to recognize, if not duplicity, at least wishful thinking; but, if the ratio of 3 : 5 = 5 : 8 is only an approximation to that of the golden section, and if the ideal measurement of Palladio's rooms does not concur with what is their actual size,[11] this is to be expected and it should not be considered useful to enlarge upon these inconsistencies. Instead it should be considered much more opportune to examine Palladio's preference for the triple division and Le Corbusier's propensity to divide by four.

At the Malcontenta, as already noticed, the facades are divided vertically into three principal fields, those of the portico and the flanking walls, and horizontally the same situation prevails in the sequence, basement, *piano nobile*, attic; but at Garches, in spite of the comparable structural *parti*, it is always a situation if not of one, at least of two or, alternatively, of four fields of interest with which we are presented. Thus in the entrance elevation, it is a business of four and one which prevails; and, in the garden facade, this breakdown becomes a matter of four and two.

But, in both houses, there are elaborations in detail of the dominant schema which becomes complicated by its interplay with a subsidiary system. That is: it is by vertical extension into arch and vault, diagonal of roof line and pediment that Palladio modifies the geometrical asperities of his cube; and this use of the circular and pyramidal elements with the square seems both to conceal and to amplify the intrinsic severity of the volumes. However, the arch, the vault, and the pyramid are among the prerogatives of solid wall construction. They are among the freedoms of the traditional plan, the *"plan paralysé"*; and the introduction of arched forms and pitched roofs is a liberty which at Garches Le Corbusier is unable to allow himself. For in the frame building it is obviously not, as in the solid wall structure, the vertical planes which predominate. Rather it is the horizontal planes of floor and roof slabs (Plate 12); and, therefore, the quality of paralysis which Le Corbusier noticed in the plan of the solid wall structure is, to some extent, transferred in the frame building to the section. Perforation of floors, giving a certain vertical movement of space, is possible; but the sculptural quality of the building as carving has disappeared and there can be nothing of Palladio's firm sectional transmutation and modeling of volume. Instead, following the predominant planes of the slabs, in the frame building extension and elaboration must occur horizontally. In other words, free plan is exchanged for free section; but the limitations of the new system are quite as exacting as those of the old; and, as though the solid wall structure has been turned on its side, with the former complexities of section and subtleties of elevation now transposed to plan, there may be here some reason for Palladio's choice of plan and Le Corbusier's choice of elevations as being the documents, in each case, most illustrative of elementary mathematical regulation.

The spatial audacities of the Garches plan continue to thrill; but it may sometimes seem to be an interior which is acceptable to the intellect alone—to the intellect operating from within a stage vacuum. Thus there is at Garches a permanent tension between the organized and the apparently fortuitous. Conceptually, all is clear; but, sensuously, all is deeply perplexing. There are statements of a hierarchical ideal; there are counter statements of an egalitarian one. Both houses may seem to be apprehensible from without; but, from within, in the cruciform hall of the Malcontenta, there is a clue to the whole building; while, at Garches, it is never possible to stand at any point and receive a total impression. For at Garches the necessary equidistance between floor and ceiling conveys an equal importance to all parts of the volume in between; and thus the development of absolute focus becomes an arbitrary, if not an impossible, proceeding. This is the dilemma propounded by the system; and Le Corbusier responds to it. He accepts the principle of horizontal extension; thus, at Garches central focus is consistently broken up, concentration at any one point is disintegrated, and the dismembered fragments of the center become a peripheral dispersion of incident, a serial installation of interest around the extremities of the plan.

But it is now that this system of horizontal extension which is *conceptually* logical comes up against the rigid boundary of the block which, almost certainly, is felt to be *perceptually* requisite;[12] and, consequently, with horizontal extension checked, Le Corbusier is obliged to employ an opposite resource. That is, by gouging out large volumes of the block as terrace and roof garden, he introduces a contrary impulse of energy; and by opposing an explosive moment with an implosive one, by introducing inversive gestures alongside expansive ones, he again makes simultaneous use of conflicting strategies.

By its complexities, the resultant system (or symbiosis of systems) throws into intense relief the elementary, geometrical substructure of the building; and, as a sequel, the peripheral incident which substitutes for the Palladian focus can also become compounded with the inversions (of terrace and roof garden) which represent an essentially analogous development to Palladio's strategy of vertical extension.

Finally, a comparable process to that which occurs in plan takes place also in the elevations, where there is the same regular diffusion of value and irregular development of points of concentration; and here, with the horizontal windows conveying an equality to both the center and verge of the facades, a disintegration of focus which is never complete causes a brisk oscillation of attention. Here, as in the plan, there is nothing residual, nothing passive, nothing slow moving; and the extremities of the block, by this means, acquire an energetic clarity and tautness, as though they were trying to restrain the peripheral incident from flying out of the block altogether.

A detailed comparison is less easy to sustain between the two houses which, initially, seemed to invite their linking together: the Savoye House and the Villa Rotonda; and, conceivably, this is because neither of these buildings is so entirely condensed in its structure and its emotional impact as are, respectively, the earlier Garches and the later Malcontenta. The Savoye House and the Rotonda are both more famous; but they are also, in each case, more obviously Platonic and easy to take. Possibly this is because they are both in the round; and that, therefore, what is concentrated in two fronts at Garches and the Malcontenta is here diffused through four, resulting in far greater geniality of external effect. But, if there is a noticeable easiness and lack of tension to be found in these facades, there are analogous developments to those in the other houses. Such are Palladio's concern, both in plan and elevation, with central emphasis and Le Corbusier's determined dispersal of focus. At Poissy, just possibly, the complicated volumes of the upper roof garden replace the Palladian pitched roof and cupola; and again, just possibly, Palladio's four projecting loggias are subsumed within the block as the enclosed terrace which, alternatively, as the dominant element of the *piano nobile*, could also be considered to correspond to the domed salon of the Rotonda.

But, symbolically and in the sphere of 'customary' beauty, Palladio's and Le Corbusier's buildings are in different worlds. Palladio sought complete clarity of plan and the most lucid organization of conventional elements based on symmetry as the most memorable form of order, and mathematics as the supreme sanction in the world of forms. In his own mind his work was essentially that of adaptation, the adaptation of the ancient house; and, at the back of his mind were always the great halls of the Imperial thermae and such buildings as Hadrian's villa at Tivoli. He had several schemes of archaeological reconstruction of Greek and Roman domestic buildings, based on Vitruvius and Pliny, incorporating elements which in Greek and Roman practice would have been found only in public buildings, but which he regarded as general. Indeed, Rome for him was still supremely alive; and, if the ancients had adapted the temple from the house, their large scale planning was, no doubt, similarly reflective.

Notoriously, Le Corbusier has an equal reverence for mathematics and he would appear also, sometimes, to be tinged with a comparable historicism. For his plans he seems to find at least one source in those ideals of *convenance* and *commodité* displayed in the ingenious planning of the Rococo hotel, the background of a social life at once more amplified and intimate. The French, until recently, possessed an unbroken tradition of this sort of planning; and, therefore, one may often discover in a Beaux Arts utilization of an irregular site, elements which if they had not preceded Le Corbusier might seem to be curiously reminiscent of his own highly suave vestibules and boudoirs. Le Corbusier admires the Byzantine and the anonymous architecture of the Mediterranean world; and there is also present with him a purely French delight in the more overt aspects of mechanics. The little pavilion on the roof at Garches is, at the same time, a temple of love and the bridge of a ship. The most complex architectural volumes are fitted with running water.

Geometrically, both architects may be said to have approached something of the Platonic archetype of the ideal villa to which the fantasy of the Virgilian dream might be supposed to relate; and the realization of an idea which is represented by the house as a cube could also be presumed to lend itself very readily to the purposes of Virgilian dreaming. For here is set up the conflict between the absolute and the contingent, the abstract and the natural; and the gap between the ideal world and the too human exigencies of realization here receives its most pathetic presentation. The bridging must be as competent and compelling as the construction of a well-executed fugue; and, if it may be charged, as at the Malcontenta with almost religious seriousness, or, as at Garches, imbued with sophisticated and witty allusion, its successful organization is an intellectual feat which reconciles the mind to what may be some fundamental discrepancies in the program.

As a constructor of architectural fugues, Palladio is the convinced classicist with a sixteenth century repertory of well-humanized forms; and he translates this received material with a passion and a high seriousness fitting to the continued validity that he finds it to possess. The reference to the Pantheon in the superimposed pediments of the Malcontenta, to the thermae in its cruciform salon, the ambiguity, profound in both idea and form, in the equivocal conjunction of temple front and domestic block; these are charged with meaning, both for what they are and what they signify; and their impression is poignant. By such apparatus the ancient house is not recreated, but something far more significant is achieved: a creative nostalgia evokes a manifestation of mythical power in which the Roman and the ideal are equated.

By contrast Le Corbusier is, in some ways, the most catholic and ingenious of eclectics. The orders, the Roman references, were the traditional architectural clothing of authority; and, if it is hard for the modern architect to be quite so emphatic about any particular civilization as was Palladio about the Roman, with Le Corbusier there is always an element of wit suggesting that the historical (or contemporary) reference has remained a quotation between inverted commas, possessing always the double value of the quotation, the associations of both old and new context. In spite of his admiration for the Acropolis and Michelangelo, the world of high classical Mediterranean culture on which Palladio drew so expressively is largely closed for Le Corbusier. The ornamental adjuncts of humanism, the emblematic representations of the moral virtues, the loves of the Gods and the lives of the Saints have lost their former monopoly; and as a result, while allusion at the Malcontenta is concentrated and direct, at Garches it is dissipated and inferential. Within the one cube the performance attempts the Roman; but, within the other, no such exclusive cultural ideal is entertained. Instead, as the sponsors of his virtuosity, Le Corbusier largely selects a variety of hitherto undiscriminated phenomena. He selects the casual incidents of Paris, or Istanbul, or wherever it may be; aspects of the fortuitously picturesque, of the mechanical, of objects conceived to be typical, of whatever might seem to represent the present and the usable past; and all those items, while transformed by their new context, retain their original implications which signify maybe Platonic ideality, maybe Rococo intimacy, maybe mechanical precision, maybe a process of natural selection. That is, one is able to seize hold of all these references as something known; but, in spite of the new power with which they become invested, they are only transiently provocative. Unlike Palladio's forms, there is nothing final about any of their possible relationships; and their rapprochement would seem to be affected by the artificial emptying of the cube in which they find themselves located, when the senses are confounded by what is apparently arbitrary and the intellect is more than convinced by the intuitive knowledge that, despite all to the contrary, here problems have been both recognized and answered and that here there is a reasonable order.

The neo-Palladian villa, at its best, became the picturesque object in the English park and Le Corbusier has become the source of innumerable pastiches and of tediously amusing exhibition techniques; but it is the magnificently realized quality of the originals which one rarely finds in the works of neo-Palladians and exponents of 'le style Corbu.' These distinctions scarcely require insistence; and no doubt it should only be sententiously suggested that, in the case of the derivative works, it is perhaps an adherence to 'rules' which has lapsed.

Addendum 1973

Though a parallel of Schinkel with late Corbu might not be so rewarding as the comparison of early Corbu and Palladio, much the same arguments as those surfacing in this article might quite well be found developing themselves if, for the Villa Malcontenta, one were to substitute the Berlin Altes Museum and, for Garches, the Palace of the Assembly at Chandigarh. Illustrations (Plates 13-16) might suffice to make the point: a conventional classical *parti* equipped with traditional *poché* and much the same *parti* distorted and made to present a competitive variety of local gestures—perhaps to be understood as compensations for traditional *poché*.

A criticism which begins with approximate configurations and which then proceeds to identify differences, which seeks to establish how the same general motif can be transformed according to the logic (or the compulsion) of specific analytical (or stylistic) strategies, is presumably Wölflinian in origin; and its limitations should be obvious. It cannot seriously deal with questions of iconography and content; it is perhaps over symmetrical; and, because it is so dependent on close analysis, if protracted, it can only impose enormous strain upon both its consumer *and* producer. However, if one would not like to imagine oneself confronted with the results of an intensive critical workout on the *matériel* provided by the Altes Museum and the Palace of the Assembly, this reservation should not be understood as depreciating the limited value of such an exercise. For the two buildings incite comparison and can also, both of them, stimulate further parallel with certain productions of Mies van der Rohe. But, if normal intuition might suggest so much, a Wölflinian style of critical exercise (though painfully belonging to a period *c.* 1900) might still possess the merit of appealing primarily to what is visible and of, thereby, making the minimum of pretences to erudition and the least possible number of references outside itself. It might, in other words, possess the merits of accessibility—for those who are willing to accept the fatigue.

## Notes

1 Isaac Ware, *The Four Books of Palladio's Architecture*, London, 1738, p. 41.

2 Le Corbusier, *Précisions sur un état présent de l'architecture et de l'urbanisme*, Paris, 1930, pp. 136-38.

3 Ware, p. 46.

4 Ware, p. 27.

5 Le Corbusier, *Précisions*, p. 123.

6 For these particular observations I am highly indebted to Rudolf Wittkower, *Architectural Principles in the Age of Humanism*, London, 1949.

7 Sir Henry Wotton, *The Elements of Architecture*, published in John Evelyn, *Parallel of the Ancient Architecture with the Modern*, 3rd ed., London, 1723, p. xv.

8 Giacomo Leoni, *Ten Books on Modern Architecture by Leon Battista Alberti*, 3rd ed., London, 1755, p. 196.

9 Le Corbusier and Pierre Jeanneret, *Oeuvre complète 1910-1929*, 3rd ed., Zurich, 1943, p. 144. These remarks refer to Garches.

10 "The break away from the laws of harmonic proportion in architecture" is extensively discussed in Wittkower (*see* n. 6), but the parallel disintegration of the Platonic-Aristotelian critical tradition is somewhat more laconically observed by Logan Pearsall Smith: "There are great youths too whose achievements one may envy; the boy David who slew Goliath and Bishop Berkeley who annihilated, at the age of twenty five, in 1710, the external world in an octavo volume; and the young David Hume, who, in 1739, by sweeping away all the props of the human understanding, destroyed for ever and ever all possibility of knowledge." Logan Pearsall Smith, *All Trivia*, London, 1947, p. 159.

11 For the actual rather than the ideal internal measurements of the Malcontenta see Ottavio Bertotti Scamozzi, *Les batiments et les desseins de andre palladio*, Vicenza, 1776-83.

12 It is possible to suppose that the rigid boundaries of Garches were considered to be perceptually necessary. The house is presented as one of 'the four compositions' in *Oeuvre complète 1910-1929*, p. 189; and, in *Précisions*, p. 73, Le Corbusier writes of Garches: "Pour s'imposer à l'attention, pour occuper puissament l'espace, il fallait d'abord une surface première de forme parfaite, puis une exaltation de la platitude de cette surface par l'apport de quelges saillies ou de trous faisant intervenir un mouvement avant-arrière."

Plate 1   Villa Capra-Rotonda, Vicenza.
Andrea Palladio, *c.* 1550.

Plate 2   Villa Savoye, Poissy. Le Corbusier,
1929-31.

Plate 3   Villa Malcontenta (Villa Foscari),
Malcontenta di Mira. Palladio, *c.* 1550-60.

Plate 4   Villa Malcontenta.

Plate 5   Villa Stein, Garches. Le Corbusier, 1927.

Plate 6   Villa Stein.

Plate 7   Villa Stein. Plan.

Plate 8   Villa Malcontenta. Plan.

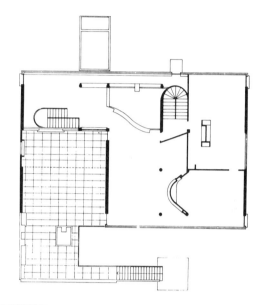

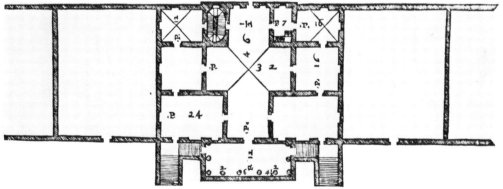

Plate 9   Villa Malcontenta. Aerial view.

Plate 10   Villa Stein. Axonometric view.

Plate 11   Villa Malcontenta. Facade.

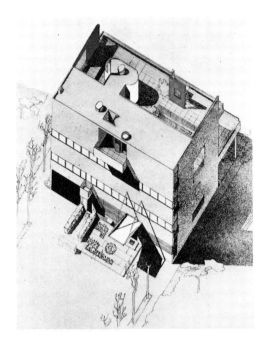

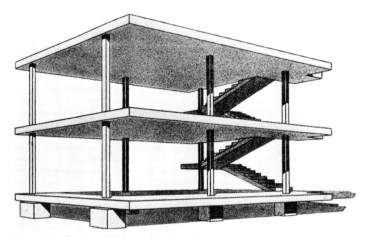

Plate 12   Project, Maison Domino. Le
Corbusier, 1914.

Plate 13   Altes Museum, Berlin. Karl
Friedrich Schinkel, 1823.

Plate 14   Altes Museum. Plan.

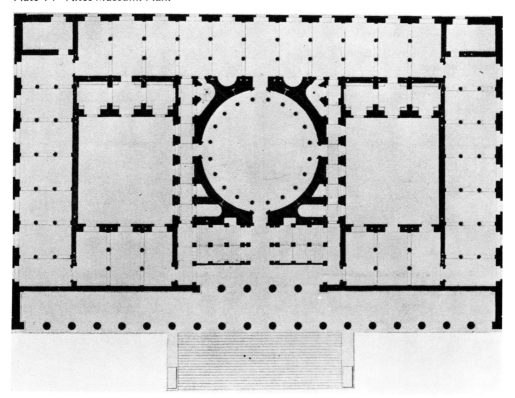

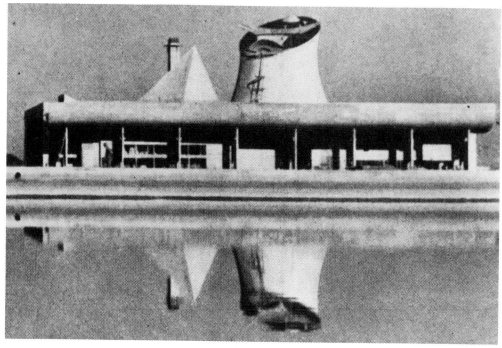

Plate 15   Palace of the Assembly, Chandigarh. Le Corbusier, 1953- .

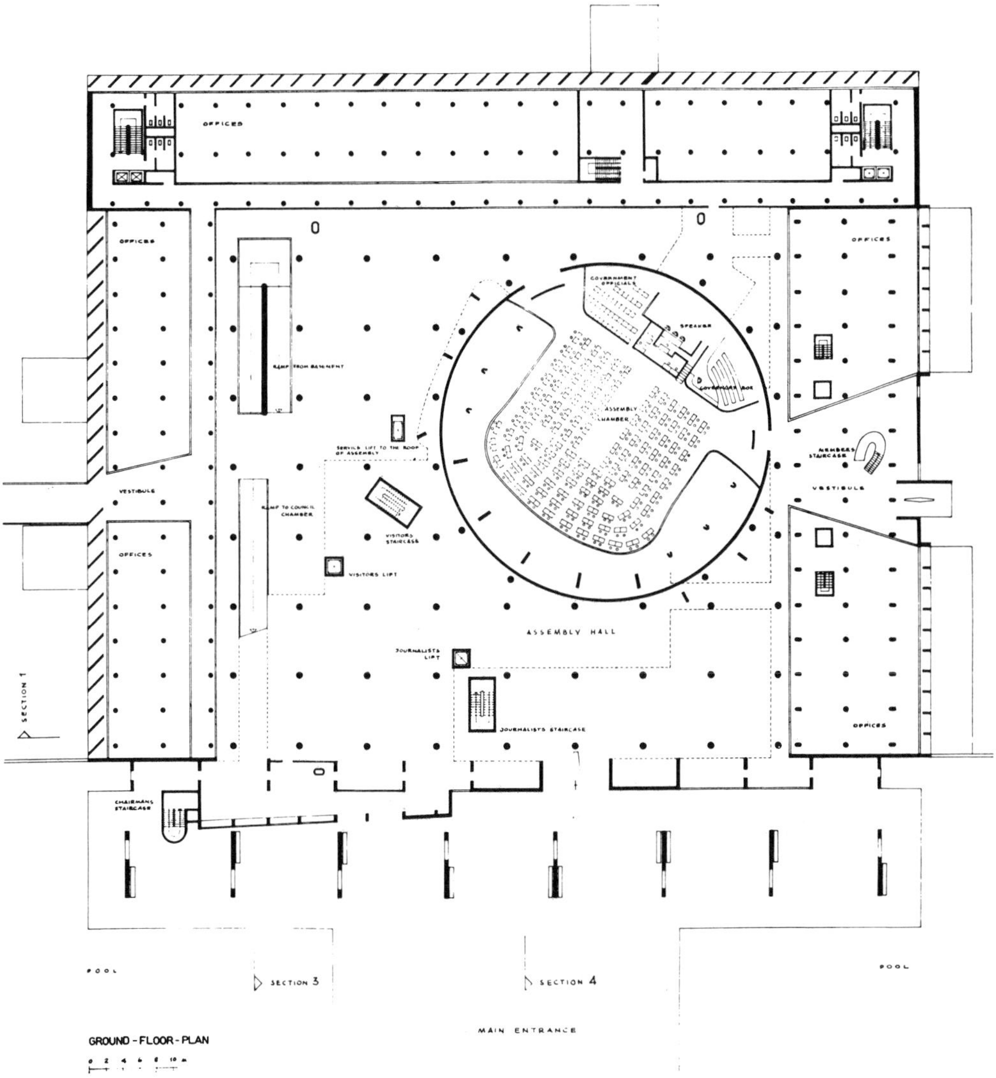

GROUND - FLOOR - PLAN

Plate 16   Palace of the Assembly. Plan.

# Mannerism and Modern Architecture

First published in the *Architectural Review*, 1950. Though this little piece, particularly in its discussion of Cubism, has been painful to me since before the day of its publication, it has here been allowed to stand substantially as published. Though a present day rehearsal of its arguments (in which I still believe) would surely employ a profoundly different strategy, because this article has long enjoyed a certain notoriety I can see no way of correcting its obscurities and maintaining its sense. Today the art historical discussion of Mannerism has achieved levels of sophistication and detachment which *c*. 1950 were simply not available; but, on the other hand, it is not evident that the modern architect's consciousness of sixteenth century themes has been considerably advanced. There are still two bodies of information—the one art historical, the other modern architectural—and the possibilities of their convergence in a work of rational exegesis still remain remote. Since the writing of this article the initiatives of Robert Venturi have, to some extent, illuminated the situation. Nevertheless, while Venturi has been quite unabashed in his parade of elements of Mannerist origin and while, by these means, he has extended the theater of architectural discourse, the theme modern architecture and Mannerism still awaits the extended and positive interpretation which it deserves.

Le Corbusier's Villa Schwob at La Chaux-de-Fonds of 1916 (Plates 17, 18), his first considerable work to be realized, in spite of its great merits and obvious historical importance, finds no place in the collection of the *Oeuvre complète*; and its absence is entirely understandable. This building is obviously out of key with his later works; and, by its inclusion with them, the didactic emphasis of their collection might have been impaired. But the omission is all the more unfortunate, in that six years later, the building was still found sufficiently serious to be published as an exemplar of proportion and monumentality.[1]

The house is of nearly symmetrical form; and, in spite of a general lightness deriving from its concrete frame, its conventional character is fairly emphatic. The principal block is supported by flanking wings; and a central hall, rising through two stories and crossed by a subsidiary axis, establishes for the plan a simple, balanced, and basically cruciform scheme. The appearance, externally, of these same characteristics of restrained movement and rational elegance seems to invite appreciation in neo-Classical terms; and thus, while the lack of ornament with the simplified cornices suggests the influence of Tony Garnier and the expression of the concrete frame in the flanking walls indicates an obvious debt to Auguste Perret, the elliptical windows are part of the stock furniture of French academic architecture and the building as a whole—compact, coherent, and precise—is an organization which the later eighteenth century might have appreciated and a work toward which a Ledoux, if not a Gabriel, might have found himself sympathetic. One may, it is true, recognize innovation in the simplification of elements, although adequate Austrian and German precedent could no doubt be suggested; one might also perceive in the two bedroom suites of the upper floor some premonition of Le Corbusier's later spatial complexities; but, having made these observations, there is little to be found, in plan and in three elevations at least, which detracts from an almost conventional and conservative excellence.

But the fourth elevation, the entrance facade, presents quite distinct problems of appreciation. Behind its wall the presence of a staircase continued to the third floor has led to an increase in height which somewhat detaches this part of the building from the rest; and this elevation further asserts a severe distinction from the volume in its rear with which on superficial examination it seems scarcely to be related. Indeed, if its succinct, angular qualities are foreign to the curvilinear arrangements of the rest of the building, its exclusive, rectilinear, self-sufficient form seems also to deny the type of organization which reveals itself from the garden.

The flat vertical surface of the two upper floors is divided into three panels. The outer ones are narrow and pierced by elliptical lunettes, but the central one is elaborately framed, comprising an unrelieved, blank, white surface; and it is toward this surface—and accentuated by all the means within the architect's control—that the eye is immediately led. The low walls, screening service rooms and terrace, are curved inwards rising towards it; the two entrance doors prepare a duality to be resolved; the projecting marquise, with its supporting columns, completes the pregnant isolation of the upper wall; the emphatic elliptical windows increase the demand for a dominant; and, with the mind baffled by so elaborately conceived an ambiguity, the eye comes to rest on the immaculate rectangle and the incisive detail of its brick frame.

Contemplating this facade for any length of time, one is both ravished and immensely irritated. Its moldings are of an extreme finesse. They are lucid and complex. The slightly curved window reveals are of considerable suavity. They reiterate something of the rotund nature of the building behind and help to stress something of the flatness of the surface in which they are located. The contrast of wall below and above the canopy excites; the dogmatic change of color and texture refreshes; but the blank surface is both disturbance and delight; and it is the activity of emptiness which the observer is ultimately called upon to enjoy.

Since this motif, which is so curiously reminiscent of a cinema screen, was presumably intended to shock, its success is complete. For it imbues the facade with all the polemical qualities of a manifesto; and it is this blank panel with its intensifying frame which endows other elements of the facade—columns and canopy—with a staccato quality seeming to foreshadow Le Corbusier's later development. Distinct and deliberate, it draws attention to itself; and yet, without apparent content, it at once distributes attention over the rest of the house. By its conclusiveness, the whole building gains significance; but, by its emptiness, it is, at the same time, the problem in terms of which the whole building is stated; and thus, as apparent outcome of its systematically opposite values, there issue a whole series of disturbances of which it is both origin and result.

Behind the panel lies the staircase, the lighting of which it can only impair, and one must assume that an architect as apt as Le Corbusier could, had he wished, have chosen some alternative and functionally more satisfactory organization; while, even if it were to be supposed (improbable as it appears) that the framed surface was intended to receive some fresco or inscription, it is still a motif sufficiently abnormal and recondite to stimulate curiosity and to encourage a hunt for possible parallels. And here the most probable field of investigation would seem to be Italian; not that with Le Corbusier any direct derivation should be expected, but that, in general terms, he so frequently appears to be descended from the architectural traditions of Renaissance humanism.

In early Renaissance loggia and palace facades, sequences of alternating windows and panels do not appear to be uncommon. In such more frequent sequences from the sixteenth century, panels and windows acquire almost equal significance. Panels may be expressed as blank surfaces, or become a range of inscribed tablets, or again they may form the frames for painting; but whatever their particular employment may be, the alternation of a developed system of paneling, with an equally developed system of fenestration, seems always to produce complexity and duality of emphasis in a facade. This is a quality which must have given considerable pleasure to the generation of architects subsequent to Bramante; and in the pages of Serlio, for instance, panels occur in almost embarrassing profusion.[2] Sometimes they are to be found in the typical alternation, or on other occasions absorbing entire wall surfaces; in elongated form they are used to intersect two whole ranges of windows, or they may appear as the crowning motif of a triumphal arch or Venetian palace. It was probably Serlio who first employed the panel as the focus of a facade. In some cases he has groups of windows arranged on either side of this reduced but evocative form of central emphasis; but it also seems likely that in only two instances does the panel make a central appearance within an elevation so restricted as that at La Chaux-de-Fonds; and although comparisons of this sort are frequently tendentious and overdrawn, the so-called Casa di Palladio at Vicenza (Plate 19) and Federico Zuccheri's casino in Florence (Plate 20) do show a quality sufficiently remarkable to permit their interpretation as sixteenth century commentaries upon the same theme. Dating from 1572 and 1578 respectively, small houses of a personal and distinctly precious quality, it would be pleasant to assume that they represented a type, a formula for the later sixteenth century artist's house.

Palladio's building is apparently generated by the combination of a domestic facade and an arcaded loggia which, in its ornaments, assumes the role of a triumphal arch. Unlike the conventional triumphal arches of antiquity, however, a developed Corinthian superstructure is included; and although on the ground floor the two functions of the loggia as part of a house and as part of a triumphal arch are closely integrated, in itself the arch is even more intimately related to the panel formed by the Corinthian pilasters above. The breaking forward of the Ionic entablature about the arch provides a direct vertical movement through the two orders, emphasizing their interdependence, so that the panel retains the focus developed by the arch below, but seems otherwise to read as an intrusion projected upward into the *piano nobile*; and its anomalous character is further increased by details which suggest a respect for the functions of the domestic facade. Thus such a feature as the balcony rail of the windows, which emerges from behind the pilasters to appear in the panel as a continuous string course, only serves to exaggerate, as it was presumably intended it should, an already inherent duality.

It need scarcely be pointed out that we are here in the presence of a formal ambiguity of the same order as that which Le Corbusier was to provide in 1916; although in lucid, academic dress, the disturbance is less perceptible and perhaps more complete. Palladio's inversion of the normal is effected within the framework of the classical system, whose externals it appears to respect; but in order to modify the shock to the eyes, Le Corbusier's building can draw on no such conventional reference. Both state the problem of their complex duality with an extreme directness and economy of means, which, by comparison, causes Federico Zuccheri's essay in the same composition to appear at once redundant and bizarre.

Zuccheri's approach is altogether more violent, his building a *jeu d'esprit* conceived as part of a program of personal advertisement illustrating his triple profession as painter, sculptor, and architect. Unlike Palladio, his two elements of focus, the void of the entrance below and the solid of the panel above, are not placed in direct relationship; but each, as the dominant interest in strongly contrasted stone and brick surfaces, appears set within an arrangement of incident which both accentuates and diminishes its importance. Two triangles of interest are thereby established. That below is formed by the three panels with their reliefs of mathematical instruments, that above is organized by windows and niches about the central panel (in this case intended to receive a painting); and this diffused incident, which is still concentrated within strictly triangular schemes, establishes a form of composition different from Palladio's, so that, with Zuccheri, the particular ambiguity of the panel is of less importance when compared with that of the entire facade.

The composition of Zuccheri's lower wall is framed by rusticated pilasters which seem to restrict its details between quite rigid boundaries; but these pilasters receive no downward transmission of weight. Two advanced surfaces in the upper story carry a form of triglyph or bracket which seems to suggest for them a function of support; but these are then displaced by niches from the position above the pilasters which, reasonably, they might be expected to occupy, while the insertion within them of elaborately framed windows invalidates still further their apparent function. The niches in themselves, on first examination, seem to expand the interest of the upper wall and to create there the appearance of an organization as open as that of the wall below is compressed; but, within this organization it becomes clear that the different elements—niches, windows, and panels—are, in reality, crushed in the harshest juxtaposition so that, on second analysis, the contrast compels one to attribute to the supposedly compressed basement an almost classical directness and ease.

The complexities and repercussions which such schemes elicit are endless and almost indefinable; but patience, conceivably, exhausts itself in the explanation. It would seem to be abundantly clear that it is a dilemma of dual significance, a distinction between the thing as it *is* and as it *appears* which seems to haunt all these three facades; and, if Zuccheri's building by comparison with the more lucid expositions seems to be something of an exercise in genre, its second-hand qualities, perhaps, enhance its value as a document, as almost a textbook illustration of deliberate architectural derangement.

The two examples from the sixteenth century are characteristic late Mannerist schemes, the most apt registers of that alleged universal *malaise* which, in the arts, while retaining the externals of classical correctness, was obliged, at the same time, to disrupt the inner core of classical coherence.

In so-called academic or frankly derivative architecture, the recurrence in 1916 of a form of composition which, at first glance, appears intrinsically Mannerist might cause some, but perhaps not undue, surprise; but, occurring as it does in the main stream of the modern movement, it is remarkable that this blank panel motif at La Chaux-de-Fonds should not have aroused more curiosity. It is not in any way suggested that Le Corbusier's use of the blank panel is dependent on the previous instances; and it is not imagined that a mere correspondence of forms necessitates an analogous content. Such a correspondence may be purely fortuitous or it may be of deeper significance.

Apart from Nikolaus Pevsner's article "The Architecture of Mannerism" and Anthony Blunt's 1949 lecture at the Royal Institute of British Architects, Mannerism, in its accepted sense as a style, has been the subject of no popular discussion. Such discussion must obviously lie beyond the scope of the present essay which, for a frame of reference, relies to a great extent on the article and lecture just cited.[3] In the most general terms works produced between the years 1520 and 1600 are to be considered Mannerist; and it is hoped that the particular analysis of two sixteenth century schemes has provided some illustration of types of ambiguity that are characteristic.

An unavoidable state of mind, and not a mere desire to break rules, sixteenth century Mannerism appears to consist in the deliberate inversion of the classical High Renaissance norm as established by Bramante, to include the very human desire to impair perfection when once it has been achieved, and to represent too a collapse of confidence in the theoretical programs of the earlier Renaissance. As a state of inhibition, it is essentially dependent on the awareness of a preexisting order: as an attitude of dissent, it demands an orthodoxy within whose framework it might be heretical. Clearly, if, as the analysis of the villa at La Chaux-de-Fonds suggests, modern architecture may possibly contain elements analogous to Mannerism, it becomes critical to find for it some corresponding frame of reference, some pedigree, within which it might occupy an analogous position.

Among sources for the modern movement, the characteristic nineteenth century demand for structural integrity has rightly received greatest emphasis. Dependent to some extent on the technical innovations of industrialism, this demand was unexpectedly reinforced by the Revivalists, both Gothic and Greek; and it was they who transformed its original rational-empirical basis and imbued this structural impulse with a dynamic emotional and moral content, so that in this possibly fallacious version, the structural tradition has remained one of the most crude, indiscriminate, and magnificently effective forces which we have inherited from the nineteenth century.

But it remains apparent that a system of architecture cannot ever enjoy a purely material basis, that some conception of form must play an equal and opposite role; and, although formal derivations for the modern movement often seem to impose too great a strain on the imagination, at a time no more remote than the later nineteenth century it is noticeable that advanced architecture from the 1870s onward belongs to one of two discernible patterns.

The program of the first is certainly closest to our sympathy and its outlines clearest in our minds. This was the heroic process of simplification, the direct assault upon nineteenth century pastiche of a Philip Webb, a Richardson, or a Berlage; and it would seem that the central tradition of modern architecture does proceed from the personal conflict which such individuals experienced between the authorities of training and reason. Obedience to the nature of materials, to the laws of structure, consecrated by the theorists of the Gothic Revival and everywhere recognizable in the products of contemporary engineering, seemed to offer an alternative to purely casual picturesque effects; and, from within such a framework, it was felt that an architecture of objective significance might be generated. Thus for architects of this school an inevitable tension was clearly experienced between a pictorial education and the more purely intellectual demands which a structural idealism imposes; and, being trained in pictorial method but insisting on an architecture regulated by other than visual laws, their forms frequently bear all the marks of the battleground from which they had emerged.

The alternative tendency, apparently, owes nothing to this dialectic; but, equally concerned with a rational solution of the mid-nineteenth century impasse, it found in physical attractiveness its architectural ideal. Without either the former school's consistent vigor or narrow prejudice, the architects of this second school look down the perspectives of history with a liberal eye and are anxious to coordinate the ensuing suggestions. Thus, from an analysis of function, there emerged a discipline of the plan; and, from the impressions of a visual survey, that research into architectural composition which engrossed so many. Adhering to no distinct formula of revival, there is a willingness in this second school to combine motifs from different styles; and, in the resultant amalgam, they appear as 'telling' features in a composition, rather than for any further significance which they might possess. Thus we find that Norman Shaw is able to support late Gothic effects of mass with details from the school of Wren; and, when architecture is chiefly valued as a source of visual stimuli, then obviously concern will chiefly be with broad effects of movement, volume, silhouette, and relationship.

Neither of these two schools can be considered as completely independent, nor as completely unaffected by the other's activities; but, while for the one an architecture objectively rooted in structure and craftsmanship is an emotional necessity, the other neither finds such objectivity possible, nor perhaps desirable. For the first school, architecture still possessed a certain moral quality—among its purposes was that of imparting a truth; for the second, the significance of architecture was more exclusively aesthetic—its purpose was to convey a sensation. The architects of this second school saw the possibilities of a rational manner to lie in the expression of the sensuous content common to all phases of art; and, in this emphasis, they are perhaps the more typical of the later nineteenth century.

The great distinction of this period, its insistence on purely physical and visual justification for form, appears to separate its artistic production from that of all previous epochs—from the Renaissance by its failure to represent public ideas, from the later eighteenth and early nineteenth century Romantic phase by its elimination of private literary flavor. For, although in intention, the architecture of the early nineteenth century was pictorial, in practice, particularly through its neo-Classical exponents, who have with justice been interpreted as the legatees of the Renaissance tradition, it inherited a good deal of earlier academic thought.

But, for the later nineteenth century, the Renaissance is no longer a positive force but a historical fact; and it is by the absence of the Renaissance theoretical tradition, with its emphasis upon other values than the visual, that particularly the academic productions of this time are most clearly distinguished.

Just as the Renaissance, in opposition to the eighteenth and nineteenth centuries, conceives Nature as the ideal form of any species, as a mathematical and Platonic absolute whose triumph over matter it is the purpose of art to assist; so, in painting, it seeks an infallibility of form. Scientific perspective reduces external reality to a mathematical order; and, in so far as they can be brought into this scheme, the 'accidental' properties of the physical world acquire significance. Therefore the artistic process is not the impressionistic record of the thing seen; but is rather the informing of observation by a philosophical idea; and, in Renaissance architecture, imagination and the senses function within a corresponding scheme. Proportion becomes the result of scientific deduction; and form (by these means appearing as a visual aspect of knowledge and typifying a moral state) acquires the independent right to existence, apart from the sensuous pleasure which it might elicit.

It was not until the later eighteenth century that, with the empirical philosophy of the Enlightenment, there emerged its corollary: the direct pictorial approach to architecture and its evaluation according to its impact on the eye. When Hume was able to declare that "all probable knowledge is nothing but a species of sensation," the possibilities of an intellectual order seem to have been demolished; and when he could add that "Beauty is no quality in the things themselves" but "exists merely in the mind which contemplates and each mind perceives a different beauty,"[4] then empiricism, by emancipating the senses, appears to have provided the stimulus and the apologetic of the great nineteenth century free-for-all. Eclecticism and individual sensibility emerged as necessary by-products; and personal liberty was as effectively proclaimed for the world of forms as, in 1789, it was asserted for the political sphere. But, just as politically the *ancien régime* lingered on, so with earlier attitudes persisting, the Romantics saw indirectly according to the associational value of their forms; and it was not until the *furore* of the movement had spent itself that late nineteenth century 'realism' came to regularize the situation.

After the mid-nineteenth century, perhaps because Liberalism and Romanticism were no longer in active and revolutionary coalition, that moral zeal which had once infused their joint program is less frequently found; and, in all activities, the attempt now seems to have been made to systematize the Romantic experience, to extract 'scientific' formulae from its subjective enthusiasms. Thus, in architecture, the Romantic forms and their *sensational* implications become progressively codified; and, while the earlier phase had been sensible of literary and archaeological overtones, for the later these suggestions tend to be discounted. An eclectic research into elements and principles of architecture now arises which is distinguished from the analyses of the Renaissance theorists by its exclusively functional and visual frames of reference.

The development of the idea of architectural composition might be cited as typical of these generalizations. The conception of architectural composition was never, during the Renaissance, successfully isolated; and, while a Reynolds and a Soane were alive to the scenic possibilities of architecture, architectural composition as such does not play a large part in their theory. A developed literature upon the subject is of comparatively recent growth; and, as representing the coordination of a subjective point of view, the idea seems to be characteristic of the later nineteenth century.

Apart from an expressed antagonism to the exponents of late nineteenth century theory, modern architects have still not clarified their relationship to its ideas; and, although these ideas now usually called academic have never been effectively replaced, modern architects generally have expressed a decisive but undefined hostility towards them. "Moi je dis oui, l'académie dit non," Le Corbusier inscribes a drawing; and, in the same spirit, functional, mechanical, mathematical, sociological arguments have all, as extra-visual architectural sanctions, been introduced to provide counter-irritants. But a mere reaction from a system of ideas is scarcely sufficient to eradicate that system; and, more than likely, in the sense of providing a matrix, the dominant attitudes of the late nineteenth century were historically effective in the evolution of the modern movement.

It is a defect of the pictorial approach, which takes account chiefly of masses and relationships in their effect upon the eye, that frequently the object itself and its detail suffer a devaluation. Subjected exclusively to the laws of human sensation, the object is seen in impressionist manner and its inner substance, whether material or formal, remains undeveloped. It is a defect of universalized eclecticism that it must inevitably involve a failure to comprehend both historical and individual personality. Its theorists perceive a visual common denominator of form but are unable to allow the non-visual distinctions of content; and thus, indisposed to permit the internal individuality of particular styles, but affirming the ideal of stylistic reminiscence, the late nineteenth century academy destroys the logic of the historical process while it insists on the value of historical precept.

By all-inclusive tolerance history is neutralized and the reduced effects of the eclectic method are rationalized in order to support a more abstract investigation of sensuous properties in mass and proportion. Thus, almost by negative action, a most powerful solvent of revivalism is provided; and in advanced circles, by the early twentieth century, with the identity of the past destroyed and revivalist motifs reduced to a mere suggestion, there is in general circulation a developed and systematic theory of the effects of architecture upon the eye.

With this conception the Art Nouveau and the more expressionist schools of contemporary architecture could certainly be associated; and, in their direct sensory appeal, those Mendelsohn sketches representing film studios, sacred buildings, observatories and automobile chassis factories,[5] might be considered a logical conclusion of the idea of architecture as pictorial composition. Within the terms of this tradition it seems probable that advanced architects of the structural tradition came to interpret the formal suggestions of 'the styles'; and, for instance, in Philip Johnson's monograph, there is clearly demonstrated the partial dependence of Mies van der Rohe's early designs on the works of Schinkel. But, if schemes of Gropius have suggested a descent from the same sources, it should be noticed that this early twentieth century admiration for neo-Classicism was not exclusive to the modern movement, for so many commercial palaces and domestic monuments betray the same affinity. In these buildings, although attempts are made to enforce classical detail, the necessarily increased scale or elaborated function leads either to inflation or towards a too discreet suggestiveness; and it is in reproducing the blocking, the outline, the *compositional* elements that the greatest success seems to have been experienced.

The Edwardian baroque, in fact, offers admirable examples of the impressionist eye brought to bear upon the remnants of the classical tradition; but, outside these strictly academic limits, we find architects functioning within the structural tradition whose point of view also remains decisively impressionist. And thus, for instance, with the early Gropius, a compositional norm rather broadly derived from neo-Classicism is actively balanced by the promptings of a mechanized structure.

As arising from such an antithesis between newly clarified conceptions of vision and structure those early twentieth century buildings which are rightly considered to belong to the modern movement can be understood, for, by other means, it seems difficult to account for the stylistic differences which separate the works of these years from those which appeared in the 1920s. The buildings of Perret, Behrens, Adolf Loos, to name architects illustrated by Nikolaus Pevsner in his *Pio-*

*neers of Modern Design*, are not naive, nor primitive; and they are evidently pre-
cursors of the later development. But, comparing, for instance, the Adolf Loos
Steiner House of 1910 in Vienna (Plate 21) with any typical production of the
twenties, it becomes clear that here there are differences of formal ideal which
neither nationality, nor the temperament of the architect, nor technical innovation, nor the maturing of an idea, can fully explain.

Loos, with his fanatical attacks upon ornament, might possibly, from one point
of view, be considered as already showing Mannerist tendencies; but, allowing for
an elimination of extraneous detail and for a certain mechanistic excellence, this
house with its extreme severity and "its unmitigated contrast of receding centre
and projecting wings, the unbroken line of the roof, the small openings in the
attic,"[6] even in the horizontal windows, is not entirely remote from the more
naked types of neo-Classical villa as projected by Ledoux. Without injustice it can
be evaluated by the pictorial criteria which we have discussed; and, although a
later nineteenth century academician might not have been overjoyed by the contemplation of this facade, there is nothing here to which he could have raised final
theoretical objection.

But, such is certainly not the case with the villa at La Chaux-de-Fonds.

A work of art lives according to the laws of the mind, and some form of abstraction clearly must form a basis for all artistic achievement; but it is apparent that,
over and above this minimum, a work may possess those specifically cerebral qualities to which the term 'abstract' is more conveniently applied, and it has, in this
sense, been commonly employed in the definition of the Cubist and subsequent
schools of painting. The Cubist experiment—which can now be seen not as an
arbitrary break with tradition, but as the necessary development of an existing
situation—is the single most striking artistic event of the early twentieth century.
Its influence and that of abstract painting in general upon the modern movement
in architecture have been consistently emphasized, and their effects are obvious:
simplification and intersection, plane as opposed to mass, the realization of prism-
like geometrical forms; in fact the developed manner of the modern movement in
the twenties. But it is clear too that, although working with a visual medium, the
abstract art of today is working with a not wholly visual purpose. For abstraction
presupposes a mental order of which it is the representative.

Here it is important to distinguish between the process of abstraction in the
Renaissance and at the present day. Abstraction occurring in Renaissance art
makes reference to a world of ideal forms, asserts what the artist believes to be

objective truth, and typifies what he considers to be the scientific workings of the universe. Abstraction in contemporary art makes reference to a world of personal sensation and, in the end, typifies only the private workings of the artist's mind.

There is thus, in both cases, a reluctance merely to report the outward forms of the external world; but, in the one, it is related to a world of public, in the other, of private symbolism. And that private symbolism might form a basis for art is clearly a point of view inherited from the subjective attitudes of developed Romanticism. Thus while, on the one hand, contemporary painting, in abandoning the impressionist program, denies the value of sensational schemes which had developed since the eighteenth century, on the other, it affirms an attitude derived from closely related sources.

This reaction to sensation, at the same time positive and negative, is as characteristic of the output of our own day as it is of certain works of the sixteenth century; and the analogy of the development in painting might conveniently be applied to architecture. Here one might notice how characteristic are Le Corbusier's reactions towards the intellectual atmosphere of 1900. His *Oeuvre complète* is a production as developed and as theoretically informed as any of the great architectural treatises of the sixteenth century; and his published writings form perhaps the most fertile, suggestive and exact statement of a point of view which has emerged since that time. Contradictions in a work of this scale are inevitable; and they are public property. It is not these which require exposition; but rather it is those more specific contradictions which emerge vis-à-vis the pictorial, rationalistic, universalized premises of the opening century.

In affirming, through the medium of abstraction, a mental order, Le Corbusier immediately dissents from the theory of rationalized sense perception which was current in 1900; but, disgusted by the inflated insipidity of Beaux Arts practice, he yet inherits its whole rationalized position in connection with the 'styles.' The notes of travel from his student sketch book represent an eclectic principle which that institution would have fully endorsed. There is here a fine lack of distinction which only the liberalism of the late nineteenth century could have permitted; and, although each example is experienced with a passion of personal discovery, this is still the characteristic theoretical program of the time. The Venetian Piazzetta, Patte's *Monuments Erigés à la Gloire de Louis XV*, the forum of Pompeii and the temples of the Acropolis, offer the material for a deduction of the bases of civic space; while impressions of Stamboul, Paris, Rome, Pisa, and the temples of Angkor Wat are jostled alongside notes from the plates of Androuet du Cerceau—apart from the later nineteenth century, no other phase in history could, with so magnificent a lack of discrimination, have comprised so wide a field.

But, if *Towards a New Architecture* is read from time to time and the reader can avoid being absorbed by the persuasiveness of its rhetoric, a fundamental dilemma becomes evident. This is the incapacity to define an attitude to sensation. An absolute value is consistently imputed to mathematics, which is 'sure and certain,' and order is established as an intellectual concept affirmative of universal and comforting truths; but, perhaps, even with the word 'comforting' the senses are involved, and it becomes apparent that cubes, spheres, cylinders, cones, and their products are demanded as objects governed by and intensifying sensuous appreciation. At one moment, architecture is "the art above all others which achieves a state of Platonic grandeur";[7] but, at the next, it becomes clear that this state, far from being changeless and eternal, is an excitement subsidiary to the personal perception of "the masterly, correct and magnificent play of masses brought together in light."[8] So the reader can never be clear as to what conception of rightness the word 'correct' refers. Is it an idea, apart from, but infusing the object, which is 'correct' (the theory of the Renaissance); or is it a visual attribute of the object itself (the theory of 1900)? A definition remains elusive.

Mathematics and geometry are, of course, not the only standards which Le Corbusier erects against the theory of the Beaux Arts and 1900. *Towards a New Architecture* proposes programs of social realism, by means of which architecture, generated by function, structure, or technique, is to acquire an objective significance as symbolizing the intrinsic processes of society. But it also becomes clear that, for reasons of a lurking indecision, the essential 'realism' of these programs cannot be converted into any system of public symbolism and that the attempt to assert an objective order appears fated largely to result in an inversion of the aestheticism which was, in the first case, so much deplored. That is: the mathematical or mechanical symbols of an external reality are no sooner paraded than they are absorbed by the more developed sensuous reaction which they provoke; and abstraction, far from abetting public understanding, seemingly confirms the intensification of private significance.

This spectacle of self-division is not peculiar to Le Corbusier. For, in varying degrees, it is a dilemma which the whole modern movement appears to share; and, in it, the mental climate of the sixteenth century receives its clearest parallel at the present day. Internal stylistic causes for sixteenth century Mannerism seem chiefly to lie in the impossibility of maintaining the majestic balance between clarity and drama which had marked the mature style of Bramante; but external factors of schism are also represented and Mannerism's architectural progress is, to a great extent, determined by those religious and political conflicts which devastated contemporary Europe. The Reformation and Counter-Reformation emphasis of religious values opposed to those of the humanists; the threat to the Papacy and the European schism which the Reformation itself elicited; the resultant increase of Spanish influence in Italy; all both represent and contribute to the emotional and intellectual disturbance. And if in the sixteenth century Mannerism was the visual index of an acute spiritual and political crisis, the recurrence of similar propensities at the present day should not be unexpected nor should corresponding conflicts require indication.

In an architectural context, the theory of 1900 might be interpreted as a reflection of the tolerant liberalism of that period; and, in our own inability to define our position toward it, we might observe that contempt which we often feel for the nineteenth century liberal's too facile simplifications. Eclecticism is essentially the liberal style; and it was eclecticism which created that characteristic product, the detached and sophisticated observer. A personality of enormous and almost mythical benevolence and goodwill, this is an individual who seems to be in fairly constant demand by the modern movement—the *ville radieuse* exists for him to enjoy; but this city also embodies a society in which it seems likely that his detached observation could have scarcely any place.

It is, conceivably, from the presence of conflicts such as these that the drama of Le Corbusier's architecture derives; and, while the villa at La Chaux-de-Fonds might be presented as a first step in such a process of inversion, it would perhaps be more opportune to return to the distinction between the modern movement before 1914 and the modern movement in the 1920s.

In his *Space, Time and Architecture*, Siegfried Giedion makes a comparison between Gropius's Bauhaus building of 1926 and a Cubist head, Picasso's *L'Arlesienne* of 1911-12 (see Plates 66 and 67); and, from it, he draws an inference of which the attractiveness cannot be denied. In the Bauhaus "the extensive transparent areas, by dematerializing the corners, permit the hovering relations of planes and the kind of overlapping which appears in contemporary painting."[9] But if, as already suggested, the program of Cubism is not wholly a visual one, are we to assume that these works, apart from a similarity of form, are animated by a deeper similarity of content? If so, we shall be obliged to admit that Gropius's aims are partly independent of visual justification; if not, we shall be obliged to deduce that, either the comparison is superficial, or that Gropius himself had not fully understood the significance of Cubism; and, of these conclusions, it is surely the first which demands our assent.

A professed lack of interest in formal experiment and a belief in the possibility of extracting an architectural lyricism from the application of rational techniques to the demands of society, appear to form the bases of Gropius's system. Yet Giedion's comparison between the Bauhaus and the Picasso shows that in Gropius's work of 1926 abstraction is not wholly denied; and it is indisputably this 'abstract' element which most clearly separates the Bauhaus from the productions previous to the First World War.

Apart from Gropius's Ahlfeld factory, the building for the Deutsche Werkbund exhibition of 1914 represents one of the most self-conscious pre-World War I attempts to extract architectural feeling from a building's structural skeleton. Specific architectural effects of the past make the slightest contribution and detail is reduced to the simplest geometrical form; but, although in this building, mass is contracted to an ultimate limit, there appears to be no decisive break with the pictorial ideals of c. 1900. The motif of the famous staircases, corner cylindrical elements which appear as wrapping round or bursting through flat facades, can be paralleled in academic architecture before this date; and, although the transparent volumes of this building represent a supreme affirmation of a mechanistic idealism, they contain in themselves no single element which appears to contradict the dominant academic theory. The famous element of space-time does not enter into this building; and, unlike the Bauhaus, its complex can be summed up from two single positions.

Even as late as 1923, the experiment at Haus Am Horn at Weimar (Plate 22), a simple composition of geometrical masses, can still be interpreted in these same terms; and a parallel with a neo-Classical monument, Goethe's garden house, could still be maintained.[10] But, in the same year, certain Bauhaus schemes—most notably those of Farkas Molnar (Plate 23)—do suggest the approach which has come to be considered as characteristic of modern architecture. In these we notice an abandoning of the idea of mass, a substitution of plane, an emphasis upon the prismatic quality of the cube; and at the same time an attack on the cube, which by disrupting the coherence of its internal volume, intensifies our appreciation of both its planar and its geometrical qualities. These are projects which appear as complete illustrations of the Giedionesque concept of space-time for which the Bauhaus is so justly famous. They are compositions which "the eye cannot sum up . . . at one view"; which "it is necessary to go around on all sides, to see . . . from above as well as from below."[11]

Now, in itself, the idea of physical movement in the observation of a building is not new; and, if it formed a typical Baroque means for observing the rise and fall of masses, it is even more apparent in the irregular schemes of Romanticism. However, even they, let alone such symmetrical compositions as Blenheim, are usually provided with a single dominant element; and, seen through the media of distance and atmosphere, the interrelationship of freely disposed masses is combined as a picturesque whole. It is clear that, though intellectual limitations do not enter into the megalomania of a Fonthill, the limitations of the eye, of human vision, are scrupulously observed.

But at the Bauhaus, while one registers mental appreciation of both plan and structure, the eye is faced with the disturbing problem of simultaneous impact from widely dispersed elements. A dominating central element is eliminated; subsidiary elements are thus unable to play a supporting role; and, in a state of visual autonomy, they are disposed around the void of the central bridge which neither provides visual explanation for them as a consistent scheme nor allows them to assume independence as separate units (Plate 24). In other words, with focus disallowed, the eye becomes stretched; and, noticing this, it might be suggested that the role of this bridge—as the fundamental core of the conception and as the negation of the visual function of a central element—is closely related to that of the blank panel at La Chaux-de-Fonds. For, in a similar way, this bridge is both a source and a result of peripheral disturbances; and it is significant that only from a non-visual angle, the 'abstract' view from the air, can the Bauhaus become intelligible to the eye (Plate 25).

In this idea of disturbing, rather than providing immediate pleasure for the eye, the element of delight in modern architecture appears chiefly to lie. An intense precision or an exaggerated rusticity of detail is presented within the bounds of a strictly conceived complex of planned obscurity; and a labyrinthine scheme is offered which frustrates the eye by intensifying the visual pleasure of individual episodes, in themselves only to become coherent as the result of a mental act of reconstruction.

Sixteenth century Mannerism is characterized by similar ambiguities; and, to proceed to comparison, a deliberate and insoluble spatial complexity might be thought to be offered equally by Michelangelo's Cappella Sforza (Figure 3) and Mies van der Rohe's project of 1923 for the Brick Country House (Figure 4).

In the Capella Sforza, Michelangelo, working in the tradition of the centralized building, establishes an apparently centralized space; but, within its limits, every effort is then made to destroy that focus which such a space demands. Invaded by columns set on the diagonal, supported by apses of a form both definite and incomplete, the central space is completed not by a dome but by a balloon vault;

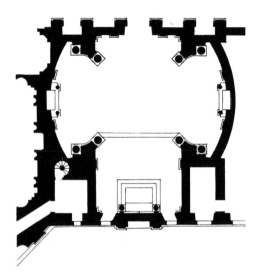

Figure 3   Capella Sforza, Santa Maria Maggiore, Rome. Plan. Michelangelo Buonarotti, completed 1573.

Figure 4   Project, Brick Country House. Ludwig Mies van der Rohe, 1923.

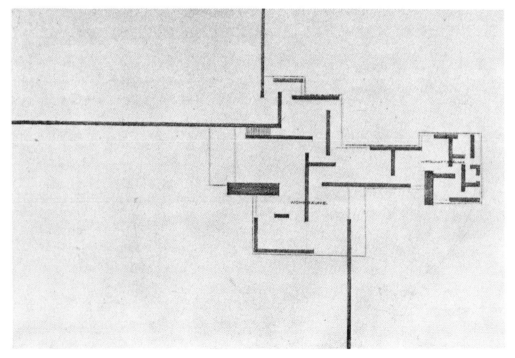

Figure 5   Project, Hubbe House, Magdeburg.
Mies van der Rohe, 1935.

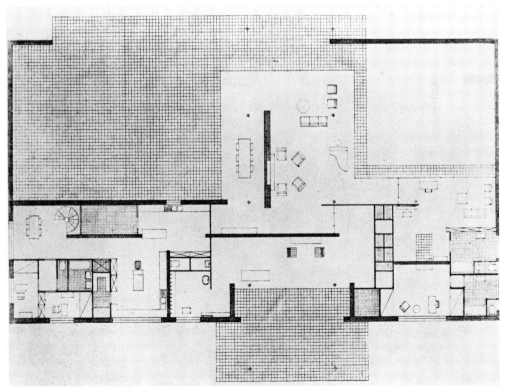

Figure 6    Villa Giulia, Rome. Plan. Jacopo
Barozzi da Vignola and Bartolomeo Amma-
nati, 1552– .

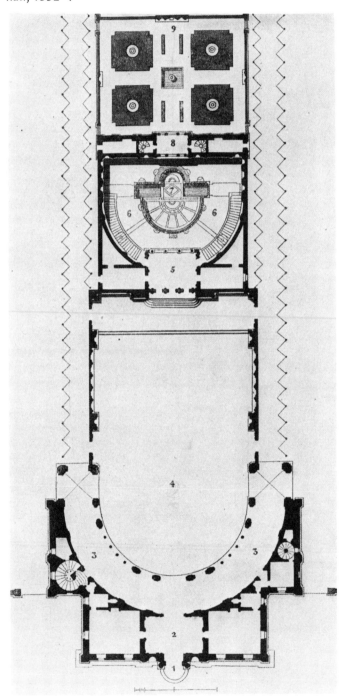

and, with this space furrowed by conflicting thrusts and engaged in active competition with the area of the sanctuary, there ensues not so much ideal harmony as planned distraction.

And, in the Brick Country House, there are analogous developments to be observed. This house is without either conclusion or focus; and, if here Mies is operating not within the tradition of the centralized building but, ultimately, in that of the irregular and freely disposed Romantic plan, the disintegration of prototype is as complete as with Michelangelo. In both cases, forms are precise, volumes competitive and undefined; but, while an effect of studied incoherence is apparently an ideal in both cases, with Michelangelo the use of a Composite order and its accessories offers a statement of conventional legibility; whereas Mies can intrude no such directly recognizable material. Mies's means are both less and less public; and, with him, the involuted clarity of his intention is, primarily, registered in the private abstraction of his plan.

Similar correspondences are to be found in two such widely differing schemes as those of the Mies project of 1935 for the Hubbe House at Magdeburg (Figure 5) and the Villa Giulia of Vignola and Ammannati (Figure 6); and, although in neither of these is there the exaggerated complexity of the last two examples, both are developed within the bounds of a tightly defined courtyard and, in neither case, are elements clearly separated or an unimpeded flow of space permitted. The general layout of the Villa Giulia is axial, emphasizing the hemicycle of its *corps de logis*; but the unifying quality of this axis is scarcely allowed to appear. As an agent of organization it is constantly interrupted by light screens and small changes of level which are sufficient to create ambiguity without making its sources in any way too obvious. At the Hubbe House, Mies imposes a T-shaped building upon his courtyard; but, like the axis at the Villa Giulia, again, its role is passive. It is both subordinate and contradictory to the rigid organization of the bounding wall; and, while the idea of the T-shape suggests a geometrical form, then by an unaccountable advance and interception of planes, the purely logical consequences of this form are studiously avoided. Thus, in both schemes, precise compositions of apparently undeniable clarity offer an overall intellectual satisfaction within which it seems neither to be desired nor expected that any single element should be visually complete.

It is particularly the space arrangements of the present day which will bear comparison with those of the sixteenth century; and, in the arrangement of facades, Mannerist parallels must be both harder to find and less valuable to prove. The Mannerist architect, working within the classical system, inverts the natural logic of its implied structural function; but modern architecture makes no overt reference to the classical system. In more general terms, the Mannerist architect works towards the crushing emphasis or the visual elimination of mass, towards the exploitation or the denial of ideas of load or of apparent stability. He exploits contradictory elements in a facade, employs harshly rectilinear forms, and emphasizes a type of arrested movement; but, if many of these tendencies are characteristic occurrences in the vertical surfaces of contemporary architecture, comparison here is perhaps of a more superficial than clearly demonstrable order.

However, in the present-day choice of texture, surface, and detail, aims general to Mannerism might possibly be detected. The surface of the Mannerist wall is either primitive or overrefined; and a brutally direct rustication frequently occurs in combination with an excess of attenuated delicacy. In this context, it is frivolous to compare the preciosity of Serlio's restlessly modeled, quoined designs with our own random rubble; but the frigid architecture which appears as the background to many of Bronzino's portraits is surely balanced by the chill of many interiors of our own day. And the linear delicacy of much contemporary detail certainly finds a sixteenth century correspondence.

A further Mannerist device, the discord between elements of different scale placed in immediate juxtaposition, offers a more valuable parallel. It is familiar as the overscaled entrance door; and it is employed, alike, by Michelangelo in the apses of St. Peter's (Plate 26) and, with different elements, by Le Corbusier in the Cité de Refuge (Plate 27). The apses of St. Peter's alternate large and small bays, and they extract the utmost poignancy and elegance from the movement of mass and the dramatic definition of plane. They are of a perfection beyond the ordinary; and, side by side with the gaping overscaled voids of window and niche in the large bays, there appears the violent discord of the smaller and dissimilar niches which seem to be crushed, but not extinguished, by the minor intercolumniations.

In comparing the apses of St. Peter's with the building for the Salvation Army, perhaps we really measure the production of our own day. In the Salvation Army building, in a composition of aggressive and profound sophistication, plastic elements of a major scale are foiled against the comparatively minor regulations of the glazed wall. Here again the complete identity of discordant objects is affirmed; and, as at St. Peter's, in this intricate and monumental conceit, there is no release and no unambiguous satisfaction for the eye. Disturbance is complete; and if, in this mechanized conception, there is nothing which replaces the purely human poetry of sixteenth century organization, there is still a savage delicacy which makes explicable Le Corbusier's *éloge* upon Michelangelo and St. Peter's which "grouped together the square shapes, the drum, the dome," and whose "mouldings are of an intensely passionate character, harsh and pathetic."[12]

The quality of this appreciation penetrates beyond the mere externals of appearance. Even in his choice of adjectives, Le Corbusier involves the observer on a plane other than that of visual discrimination; and, although such discrimination may assist the evaluation of Mannerist and modern architecture, through the standards of the eye neither can be fully understood. St. Peter's, as conceived by Michelangelo, Le Corbusier finds the embodiment of "a passion, an intelligence beyond normal, it was the everlasting Yea," an eternal scheme which is beyond the limitations of any time. But it is surely not accidental that it is by the Mannerist excess and conflict of this building that he is most deeply moved. Nor, presumably, is it by accident that this capacity of a modern architect to perceive stridently incompatible details should so closely coincide with the beginning of their investigation by historians of art.

For Burckhardt in the nineteenth century, the Ricetto of Michelangelo's Laurenziana, embodying some of his earliest Mannerist experiments, was "evidently a joke of the great master." But, for subsequent generations, the joke has become less clear; and, although for a time it was only a proto-baroque sixteenth century which was visible, for the 1920s an epoch curiously reproducing contemporary patterns of disturbance became apparent. At this time, it is as though the eye received a decisive twist by which, since it demanded visual ambiguity, it could produce it in contemporary works and discover it in a previous age—even in works of apparently unimpeachable correctness. Thus, if at one time the classicism of the whole Renaissance movement seemed to be completely clear and, if at another, the impressionist eye of the Edwardians was everywhere enabled to see the voluptuous qualities of their own baroque; so the present day seems to be particularly susceptible to the uneasy violence of Mannerism which marks both its own productions and its historical admirations. Thus, it is perhaps inevitable that Mannerism should come to be isolated and defined by historians during those same years of the 1920s when modern architecture felt most strongly the demand for inverted spatial effects.

Notes

1 In Le Corbusier's *Vers une architecture*, according to the English translation, London 1927, p. 76, "this villa of small dimensions, seen in the midst of other buildings erected without a rule, gives the effect of being more monumental and of another order."

2 See Serlio, *Tutte l'opere d'architettura*. In the edition of 1619, paneling alternating with windows occurs in Book VII, pp. 15, 23, 25, 27, 29, 33, 43, 45, 53, 151, 159, 187, 221, 229. The example in Book VII, p. 187, suggests itself as a possible source for Palladio's scheme. It was perhaps through the influence of Serlio that this motif penetrated France, where, for instance, alternating with a range of windows, it is to be seen in such a scheme as Lescot's Louvre.

3 Nikolaus Pevsner, "The Architecture of Mannerism," *Mint*, 1946. Anthony Blunt, "Mannerism in Architecture," *R.I.B.A. Journal*, March, 1949.

4 David Hume, "Of the Standard of Taste," *Essays Moral, Political and Literary*, London, 1898, p. 268.

5 See Arnold Whittick, *Eric Mendelsohn*, London, 1940.

6 Nikolaus Pevsner, *Pioneers of the Modern Movement*, London, 1937, p. 192.

7 Le Corbusier, *Towards a New Architecture*, London, 1927, p. 102.

8 *Ibid.*, p. 31.

9 Siegfried Giedion, *Space, Time and Architecture*, 5th ed., Cambridge, Mass., 1967, p. 495.

10 Herbert Bayer, Walter Gropius, Ilse Gropius, *Bauhaus, 1919-28*, New York, 1938, p. 85.

11 Giedion, p. 497.

12 Le Corbusier, *Towards a New Architecture*, p. 158.

Plate 17 Villa Schwob, La Chaux-de-Fonds.
Le Corbusier, 1916.

Plate 18 Villa Schwob. Plan.

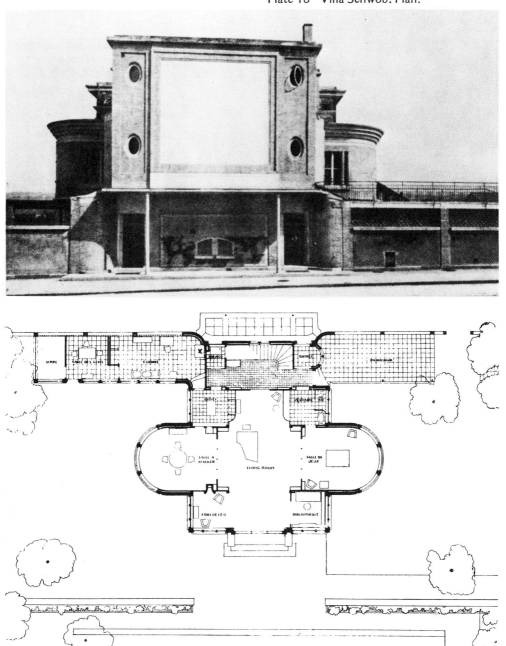

Plate 19   Casa di Palladio (Casa Cogollo), Vicenza. Attributed to Andrea Palladio, *c.* 1572.

Plate 20   Casino dello Zuccheri, Florence. Federigo Zuccheri, 1578.

Plate 21   Steiner House, Vienna. Adolf Loos, 1910.

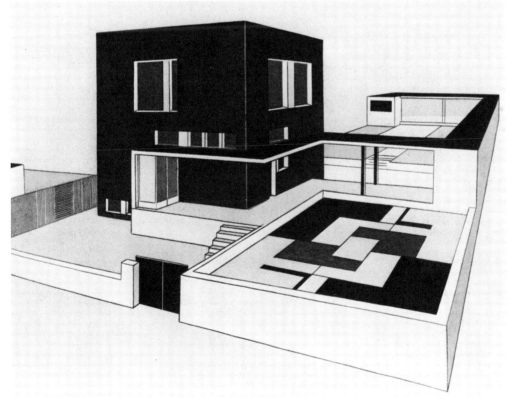

Plate 22   Haus am Horn, Weimar. Georg
Muche and Adolf Meyer, 1923.

Plate 23   Project, The Red Cube. Farkas
Molnar, 1923.

Plate 24   Bauhaus, Dessau. Walter Gropius,
1925-26.

Plate 25   Bauhaus. Aerial view.

Plate 26   St. Peter's, Rome. Detail of apses. Michelangelo Buonarotti, 1546- .

Plate 27   Cité de Refuge (Salvation Army Building), Paris. Facade. Le Corbusier, 1932-33.

Character and Composition;
or Some Vicissitudes of
Architectural Vocabulary
in the Nineteenth Century

Written, 1953-54. First published in *Oppositions 2*, 1974.

The shelves of any representative architectural library in the United States or Great Britain might suggest that between 1900 and 1930 the major critical interest of the architectural profession throughout the English speaking world lay in the elucidation of the principles of architectural composition. Certainly a surprising number of books upon this subject were published during these years, and if few have appeared since the last date, it is equally evident that very few were published before the first.

*A Discussion of Composition, Architectural Composition, The Principles of Architectural Composition*[1] —the titles are familiar and the publications, all showing allegiance to closely related critical patterns, now have a flavor of the period. The aim of such books as these was avowedly pedagogic and (using the word in no derogatory sense) their authors evidently entertained an academic ideal. Sharing a common critical vocabulary, and apparently enjoying a common visual experience, these writers felt no compulsion to lead an attack on either the present or the immediate past; and while they had no inherent connection with the modern movement in architecture, they were not always insulated from contemporary development—nor were they necessarily without enthusiasm for it. Making no overt display of bias and by no means simply committed to retrospective attitudes, they were preoccupied with the survival of certain standards of urbanity and order, certain received ideas which for them were identifiable with tradition; but above all, as the titles of their books continuously reaffirm, they were anxious to extract from historical and current precedents a formal common denominator—the quality which they recognized as *correct composition.*

These books are usually to be found in close proximity to, and often on the same shelves as the manifestos of the specifically modern movement which were published during the same years; and, apart from the obvious differences in temperature between the two styles of publication, there are other differences which invite notice. Thus the most cursory reading of any of the pronouncements of the great innovators of the 1920s suggests that for such figures as Le Corbusier, Mies Van der Rohe, and Gropius, the existence of any such *principles of composition* as the academicians presumed was not only dubious but irrelevant. These men were convinced that an authentic architecture could only be a rationalization of objective facts. One might believe that for them 'composition' implied a regard for mere appearance, had suggestions of subjectivity, of formalism—and however highly formed their buildings may have been, they were certainly unanimous in asserting their innocence of formal intention. "We refuse," writes Mies, "to recognise problems of form; but only problems of building"[2] and, even though this statement may be no more than a matter of polemics, the assertion of such opinions is enough to indicate a state of mind which could only regard the idea of composition as a discreditable one.

It is for reasons such as these that around this apparently innocent word inhibitions have gathered thick, so that except in its esoteric sense, as a reference to a composition within the post-Cubist tradition, a tendency might be noticed to use it only with considerable reserve. Sometimes indeed it is positively anathematized; and then—for instance when Frank Lloyd Wright pronounces, "Composition is dead that creation may live"[3]—there seem to be evoked echoes of similar scruples already experienced by architects and critics of the nineteenth century.

"I am always afraid to use this word composition," Ruskin announces; and when, as the major apologist of the mid-Victorian epoch he *was* obliged to use it, he guarded himself against possible misinterpretation by means of elaborate footnotes:

**The word composition has been so much abused, and is in itself so inexpressive, that when I wrote the first part of this work I intended to use in the final section of it the word 'invention' and to reserve the term composition for that false composition which can be taught on principles.[4]**

That a single word can be productive of such alternatives of damnation or involved reserve no doubt says much for the meanings with which it has been endowed; and possibly the evidence of such elaborate semantic diffidence does bring us face to face with a recurring critical dilemma, important not only to the mid-nineteenth century, but also to the present day.

At the present day the composition books are partly, but not completely, discredited; and the pronouncements of the innovators of the 1920s are partly, but not completely, accepted. Thus one group of critical standards survives with diminished prestige, while another has not achieved comprehensive definition. Modern architecture has professedly abjured composition; but the composition books recognize no situation in which their theory could become an irrelevance. The composition books are judiciously disinterested, catholic, temperate, and pragmatic; the classic manifestoes of modern architecture are partisan, exclusive, inflammatory, and doctrinaire. In any final analysis of its theory, modern architecture seems to rest upon a conviction that authentic architectural form can only be engendered by recognizing the disciplines which function and structure impose. But the authors of the composition books find that this thesis cannot engage their convictions. For them it is by no means an article of faith, rather it is an interesting supposition; and while they are indisposed to quarrel with it, they are definitely unwilling that it should form the focus of their critique. A truly significant building for these theorists is not an organization derived from functional and structural disciplines—although these may have contributed to it. But a truly significant building is preeminently a structure, organized according to *the principles of architectural composition* and infused with a symbolic content which is usually described as *character.*

According to this doctrine the presence of both good composition and appropriate character is essential in a successful building, and the presence of the one is not automatically productive of the other.

Proper character does not necessarily accompany the securing of good composition. . . . A factory may display all the correct graces of classical architecture but may look like a public library. On the other hand a church may be recognised as a church on account of the associated elements—the spire and stained glass windows—but be entirely lacking in the principles of good design. Proper character and principles of composition are not synonymous; they appear together only by a conscious effort of the designer. They must both be present in a successful piece of architecture.[5]

Character is seldom, if ever, defined, but it is generally implied that it may be at once the impression of artistic individuality and the expression, either symbolic or functional, of the purpose for which the building was constructed. Often, however, it is admitted that the presence of character has not always been a necessary attribute of architecture; and when this admission is recognized, and when it is observed that the present day has imposed critical taboos on characterization also, a further dimension to the problem is suggested. And since both words are now somewhat suspect to the strictly orthodox, their suspicions do prompt some investigation of a possible relationship and the ideas which this relationship involves.

It is clear that in the strictest meaning of the word any organization is a composition, whether 'correct' or not; it is also evident that any building will display character, whether intentionally or otherwise; but if such general definitions of both terms are to be accepted then further inquiry will be blocked, reactions such as Ruskin's or Wright's to specific meanings of the word composition will become inexplicable, and the expression of character will be assumed to represent an interest of all architects at all times.

But as might be expected, the introduction of both words into the critical vocabulary of architecture seems to have been an achievement of the eighteenth century. Certainly after 1770 both become fairly frequent, whereas before 1700 one is apt to look for either of them in vain. Thus neither Alberti, Palladio, nor the elder Blondel, to select three crucially important theorists, seem to have envisaged the working out of an architectural theme to have been a matter of informing *composition* with *character*. For them the process of design was a Vitruvian one involving 'invention,' 'compartition,' 'distribution,' 'ordinance'; while what the later eighteenth century understood as the 'arts of composition,' earlier critics usually described—with somewhat different meaning—as 'the arts of design.'

Possibly the word composition makes its first decisive English appearance with Robert Morris's *Lectures on Architecture* in 1734. "Architecture is an art useful and extensive, it is founded upon beauty, and proportion or harmony are the great essentials of its composition," writes Morris; and with this idea of a 'composed' architecture it is interesting to notice that much of what was later referred to as character is already implied, for architecture "is divided into three classes, the Grave, the Jovial, and the Charming" and "these are designed to be fitted and appropriated to the several scenes which art or nature has provided in different situations." While

A Champaign open Country requires a noble and plain Building. . . . A Situation near the Sea requires the same, or rather a Rusticity and Lowness. . . . The Cheerful Vale requires more Decoration and Dress, and if the View be long or some adjacent River runs near by it, the Ionic Order is the most proper.[6]

But in spite of Morris's example, neither composition nor character seems to have enjoyed an immediate success and it was not until the later eighteenth century with such figures as Robert Adam that the use of the first became more general. With Adam composition is associated with 'movement,' and from the preface to his *Works in Architecture* it may be seen how 'movement' was connected with the appearance of a diversified form. In his well known definition,

Movement is meant to express the rise and fall, the advance and recess, with the other diversity in form, in the different parts of a building; so as to add greatly to the *effect* of the composition.

'Movement' also serves to produce "an agreeable and diversified contour that groups and contrasts like a *picture* and creates a variety of light and shade which gives great spirit, beauty, and effect to the composition."[7] Thirteen years later in his celebrated advice to the architect Sir Joshua Reynolds gave a more august confirmation to these pictorial points of view. The architect

should take advantage *sometimes* to that which the Painter should always have his eyes open,—the use of accidents to follow where they lead, and to improve them, rather than always to look to a regular plan. . . . As buildings depart from regularity they now and then acquire something of scenery. . . .[8]

By this shifting of emphasis from the work of architecture in itself to the effect of the work upon the spectator, the late eighteenth century was able to accommodate a conspicuously dominant academic theory and a powerfully subversive undercurrent. But, however significant was the complex of new ideas which now demanded expression as 'composition,' even as late as 1806-9 Sir John Soane's *Royal Academy Lectures* still observed the standard academic pattern. In his lectures Soane very briefly alluded to the "principles of architectural composition" (the first English appearance of the term?); but for him the arbiters of architectural form still remained the orders, and the problem of architectural design a problem of ordinance.

As a kind of semi-official and perhaps retarded index to the history of ideas the articles on architecture in the earlier editions of the *Encyclopedia Britannica* may be allowed to illustrate the changing thought of this time. Thus in the first edition (1773) an unexceptionable statement of the academic position is provided. Architecture, one reads, is an art for use and ornament, and of its ornaments the column is the chief. No mention is made of 'composition,' but it is stated that architecture, being governed by proportion, "requires to be guided by rule and compass," i.e., it is a geometrical rather than a pictorial art, so that after a distribution of the elements necessary for convenience the process of architectural design becomes in theory an ordering of columns.

In the next five editions the same ideas are repeated and it is not until 1832, with the seventh edition, that there is a distinct break. Now, quite suddenly, the article is prefaced by an analysis of *"the different architectural styles,"* while its principal section consists of a discussion of what was previously taken for granted —"the elements of beauty in architecture." The specific problems of an architecture of columns have now ceased to be of absorbing interest; and significantly in their place *"the principles of composition"* have at last emerged as a predominant discipline—although at this date, unlike the early twentieth century, it was believed that no *single* set of principles was to be found. The methods of composition, it was pronounced, must differ

in the widely differing species of architecture whose tendencies in the one are to the horizontal or depressed, and in the other to the vertical or upright lines and forms. This being the case it will be necessary to treat of them separately for rules which apply to the one are totally inapplicable to the other. . . .

This final expurgation of academicism from the *Encyclopedia Britannica* (almost one might feel as a by-product of the Reform Act) did not pass unnoticed. The *Architectural Magazine*, for instance, was enthusiastic in its approval, and the *Encyclopedia* could scarcely have any longer postponed its change in tone; for by then the 'legitimate' architectural tradition which it had for so long upheld was obviously in a state of complete disintegration.

It seems to have been in the prefaces to those many early nineteenth century publications devoted to small houses and villas that the ideas were popularized to which the *Encylopedia Britannica* at last gave sanction. Throughout the books of such architects as William Atkinson, Robert Lugar, Edmund Aikin, C. A. Busby, J. B. Papworth, Francis Goodwin, and P. F. Robinson, the words 'composition,' 'character,' 'effect,' 'interest,' and 'expression' are liberally scattered; and the further these architects succeed in emancipating themselves from the Anglo-Palladian tradition, the more prone are they to the use of this new vocabulary.[9]

Lugar, for instance, speaks of "composing architectural designs for dwellings," and makes it clear that the architect "should frequently compose with a painter's eye." Busby, although he concedes that it is to the Greeks "to whom we are indebted for the three most beautiful of the orders of architecture," finds "as appears from the great similarity of their buildings," that they were "not deeply versed in composition." Aikin discovers "contrast and variety essential to architectural beauty"—they are qualities which impart "character and interest to any composition"; but he cautions that "in carrying into execution the designs of modern villas" the architect should be careful "to avoid the contrast of equal parts; to reject the square and the cube, and thus escaping monotony, the composition will acquire character and expression." Robinson from the first conceives the building itself as a picture, and for him, following Sir Uvedale Price, it is not possible that "a union of character can prevail until the principles of painting are applied to what in any way concerns the embellishment of our houses."

From this evidence it is possible to assume that the word 'composition' really entered the English architectural vocabulary as a result of the formal innovations of the Picturesque, and that it was conceived as being peculiarly applicable to the new, free, asymmetrical organizations which could not be comprehended within the aesthetic categories of the academic tradition. The comparable evolution of a similar but not identical evolution in continental Europe, which it is not proposed to trace here, was presumably more intimately involved with the whole rationale of Romantic Classicism, and seemingly the emergence of the idea of character was integral to both these developments.

The introduction into the critical vocabulary of the concept of character is generally presumed to be derived from Shaftesbury; but with the exception of Robert Morris, already noticed, English architects again seem to have been somewhat slow in applying it to their purposes. Emil Kaufmann[10] has indicated how the word early became naturalized in French architectural circles; but in England, like the complementary term composition, it seems scarcely to have made any decisive appearance until the 1790s, when curiously it has already the air of being very well established. Thus Repton in his *Sketches and Hints on Landscape Gardening* distinguishes the different *characters* of houses and grounds and presents the idea of character as a congruity of mood very much as Morris had understood it sixty years previously.[11]

And this interpretation of character was consistently echoed, as, for instance, by John Buonarotti Papworth when in his *Ornamental Gardening* he advises that if the site for a proposed house be a plain

embellished with tall aspiring trees, particularly a mixture of the pine, beech and fir, with the oak and elm, and the distant scenery composed of long ranges of lofty hills and the spires of towns and cities, the features of the architecture should be Grecian. . . . Upon similar principles if the ground be part of a hill and the forms of the trees more round, or the structure broken and romantic, the Gothic of massive or delicate forms may be used; the former where the effect is rocky, bold and prominent, and the latter where its parts are polished and refined.[12]

But this conception of character had further implications. A building should not only be animated by the mood of a landscape, but should also disclose purpose; so that in his *Rural Residences* Papworth introduces a complementary proposition that

the practice of designing the residence of a clergyman with reference to the characteristics of the church to which it belongs where the style of architecture is favourable to such selections, is desirable not only as relates to tasteful advantage; but as it becomes another and visible link between the church itself and the pastor who is devoted to its duties; and also leads the spectator very naturally from contemplating the dwelling to regard the pious character of its inhabitant.[13]

In addition to such connotations the word might be used quite indifferently as referring to a class, species, or style—buildings might show "a fancy or varied character," or might be erected in "the Gothic character"; or they might suggest a certain social expressiveness, displaying "a character becoming to an English gentleman, plain and unaffected"; but on the whole, however various might be the interpretations of character, its presence was envisaged as determined by some evident particularity. It is thus in his *Encyclopedia of Cottage Farm and Villa Architecture* that Loudon defines the term for the average naive reader of his day:

Character in architecture, as in physiognomy, is produced by the prevalence of certain distinctive features, by which a countenance or a building is at once distinguished from others of the same kind. Hence, numbers of buildings like numbers of human beings, may exist without exhibiting any marked character. On the other hand there may be buildings, which from their general proportions being exalted, and from all their parts being justly distributed, exhibit what is akin to nobleness of character. . . . In general whatever is productive of character in a building must be conspicuous and distinctive; and it should rather consist of one than many features.[14]

On the strength of such casual references it is not easy to appreciate the disruptive force with which the idea of character, throughout the late eighteenth and early nineteenth centuries, was imbued. But the demand for expressed character as a prerequisite of good architecture was perhaps the principal agent in dissolving the hierarchy of value to which the academic system had been committed. The academic tradition had been preoccupied with the ideal and with its physical embodiment as a visual norm; it had promulgated laws and had been indisposed to concern itself with exceptions to these; "the whole beauty and grandeur of art consists in being able to get above all singular forms, local customs, particularities and details of every kind,"[15] says Sir Joshua Reynolds; but it was now precisely these 'singular forms,' 'local customs,' exceptions, those accidents of which Reynolds had himself inconsistently approved, which had become full of interest and 'character'; and perhaps in no way is the Romantic revolution so completely represented as by this discovery. "The perfectly characteristic alone deserves to be called beautiful," Goethe had written. "Without character there is no beauty,"[16] and character became one of the most familiar, most repeated motifs of the new era.

Thus, and again in his academy lectures, Sir John Soane invokes the characteristic almost, one might feel, as a counter to Reynolds's earlier insistence on the ideal.

Notwithstanding all that has been urged to the contrary, be assured my young Friends [he tells his students] that Architecture in the hands of men of Genius may be made to assume whatever character is required of it. To attain this object, to produce this Variety it is essential that every building should be conformable to the uses it is intended for, and that it should express clearly its Destination and its Character, marked in the most decided and indisputable manner. The Cathedral and the Church, the Palace of the Sovereign and the dignified Prelate; the Hotel of the Nobleman; the Hall of Justice; the Mansion of the Chief Magistrate;

the House of the rich individual; the gay Theatre, and the gloomy Prison; nay even the Warehouse and the Shop, require a different style of Architecture in their external appearance. . . .[17]

And if Soane had scarcely meant that differences of character necessitated literal differences of style—as already noticed—this conception of character as a subjective expression of purpose was shortly to lead to just this idea.

The effects of this recognition of 'characteristic' beauty could obviously be illustrated by the comparison of almost any buildings of the mid-eighteenth and early nineteenth centuries, and such houses as Woolley Park (Plate 28) and Endsleigh (Plate 29) might be allowed to indicate the transformation. Thus although it would now be absurd to state that Woolley Park lacks character, it is obvious that an exhibition of character was not its architect's aim. It is an impersonal building and a critic of the early nineteenth century would not have considered it to be a 'characteristic' work—nor yet an example of 'architectural composition.' In Woolley Park the architect may be said to have been concerned not with the 'characteristic' but rather with the 'typical.' It aspires to be an ideal and a general structure, and its architect, concerned with typicality, operates within a given and known quality. The building is determined by certain irreducible formal restrictions. Such character as it does display is conventionalized and limited to the Doric mode implicit in its columnar motif, and this same motif enforces regulations which infuse the entire facade. Essentially Woolley Park is an ordinance of columns, a geometrical exercise in the consequences of bringing together columns and walls.

Endsleigh, however, is independent of any such ordinance, and its architect, emancipated from the necessities of system, inspired by a pictorial ideal, has constructed a species of architectural scenery. But it is not only in this irregular distribution, in this composition, that the house deviates from the inherited academic canon. It is more particularly by its evocative, its 'characteristic' appeal. Contemporary observers of Endsleigh undoubtedly found its quasi-Elizabethan undress, its naturalistic charm to be full of character; but almost certainly they were led to discover this same value in its roof, its chimneys, and its porch. "The porch, the veranda, or the piazza are highly characteristic features," wrote Andrew Jackson Downing of similar buildings at a somewhat later date in the United States. And again, "The prominent features conveying expression of purpose in dwelling houses are the chimneys, the windows, and the porch . . . and for this reason whenever it is desired to raise the character of a cottage or a villa above mediocrity, attention should first be bestowed on these portions of the building."[18]

Downing's dictum might be accepted as having been fundamentally of English
origin, and his "prominent features" are in fact the same character-contributing
"distinctive features" by which, to refer back to Loudon, "a countenance or a
building is at once distinguished from others of the same kind." They are at once
the expressions of purpose and the inspirations of certain less defined chains of
associations; and this Janus-like quality which they reveal, and which seems to
have been understood to be their charm, is central to the idea of character.

The cult of character was simultaneously a cult of the remote and the local, of
the very specific and the highly personal. Fundamentally it was a revolt against
the ideality of the academic tradition. The multiplicity of appearances which the
academic tradition had felt obliged to abstract to a single type was now found in
itself to be significant; and the 'characteristic' form of Endsleigh derives from an
attempt to accept this multiplicity and to give individual expression to both the
distinct attributes and the indefinite overtones assumed to be inherent to each
and every part of the building. Both functions *and* associations, since the first are
particular and the second private, were acceptable evidence of this multiplicity.
The expression of the first was the product of pragmatic argument, the expression
of the second the product of sentiment. Character was empirical and psychological and the tone of the age accepted it as at once the mark of common sense, the
sign of sincerity, and the accent of the natural man. It was, one might be disposed
to say, a democratic value; and, since certainly the idea of a constant characteristic attribute, an attribute which transcended style, offered a kind of egalitarian
common denominator for the appreciation of all styles, vernacular themes previously considered irrelevant or low could now, as at Endsleigh, achieve an architectural legitimacy, while simultaneously historical and geographical panoramas
could be opened which had previously been considered bizarre. Thus, as the
source of that extended receptiveness which distinguishes the nineteenth century,
the demand for character seems also to stand as the guarantee of its formal anarchy, for by its simple recognition, liberalized in his sympathies and enfranchised
of time, the architect was now heir to all the ages, and for him not only the whole
of nature, but the whole of history had become present—and available.

The magnitude of this revolution has perhaps been obscured by the willingness
of neo-Georgian criticism to see the Picturesque merely as a harmlessly aberrant
activity of the eighteenth century connoisseur, or alternatively as the first evidence of that decline in taste which brought all to confusion. Obviously there was
no change so abrupt as might here be implied, but by 1800 the impetus of the

new attitudes had gained in velocity, and by 1830 their success was complete.

Almost immediately, however, the new principles enjoyed the penalties of success, and as ideas generally received, they were laid open to the scepticism of the minority. The entertainment of doubt bred a conviction of error, and by the 1840s a sharp reaction was defined. Already by 1842, that most respected architectural authority, *The Ecclesiologist*, reviewing a new work on church architecture, complains that throughout the book the author lays too much stress on what he denominates 'effect,' and 'the picturesque,' 'pleasing effect,' 'proportion,' and 'varied outline.'[19] For the serious Gothic Revivalist these words were coming to imply "a painful sense of unreality,"[20] and the architect or critic who could use them could scarcely be completely aware of what a later critic called "the deep objective truth in pointed architecture."[21]

But this revulsion was not confined to the Gothic Revivalists; in 1844 C. R. Cockerell, who certainly found no "deep objective truth in pointed architecture," was equally damnatory of the eclectic picturesque, which he found to be

**"the most emasculating vice, the most uncertain treacherous *ignis-fatuus*; a principle of pseudo-life, ever without fruit or result. If the artist or life-battler would effect aught consistent or real he must work out *one* rule of action, and adhere to that and make it fruitful."[22]**

On these points, if on nothing else, *The Ecclesiologist* might well have been in complete agreement with Cockerell, since like the Gothic Revivalists he required single-mindedness and demanded something *real*. "A *real* Swiss cottage in Switzerland is as characteristic as picturesque; for this simple reason because it *is* real,"[23] *The Ecclesiologist* declares in 1846; and again in 1851 the same review finds that in the Crystal Palace, "the construction is almost entirely real, all beauty in the fabric depending on the development of that construction."[24] Architecture, according to that most literate of Gothic Revivalists, Street, is not to be judged in "a mere artistic light," but only "in proportion . . . as a work is entirely and undeniably real so essentially is it good in the first place."[25] "Rough stone walls are thoroughly good and real" he says elsewhere, and from his *Brick and Marble Architecture* it may be learned that the whole value of the middle ages lies in its "intense desire for reality and practical character."[26]

Instances of this demand for 'reality' could be multiplied; but in its consistent recurrence throughout the more self-conscious criticism of the day there may be seen the same pattern of thought which Ruskin's carefully guarded use of the term composition implies. The architects of the mid-century had reacted against their own inherited disposition to think in terms of the Picturesque; and an architecture so evolved they now believed to be logically indefensible. "There is nothing in the world so indefinable and so entirely depending on taste or caprice as what is called 'the picturesque' " is a fair sample of the attitude of *The Ecclesiologist.*[27] The Picturesque was now found to be emphasizing the pleasure of the eye, rather than the rational existence of the object. It had aimed to produce 'effect,' and, if by means of certain visual stimuli, it had induced an atmosphere in which certain states of mind were possible, its success was assured. But the mid-century architects had come to require that their visual stimuli should be capable of more rational, or at least more *mental* explanation. Picturesque phenomena could now only be offensive if not the seeming product of necessity, only meretricious if pursued for their own sake. "The true picturesque," wrote a contemporary, "derives only from the sternest utility";[28] and in this new climate of feeling, composition became a word which the semantically scrupulous were happy to neglect.

But character, on the other hand, had now acquired a new dimension of meaning.

**I recollect no instance of a want of sacred character, or of any marked and painful ugliness, in the simplest or most awkwardly built village church, where stone and wood were roughly and nakedly used,**

says Ruskin in *The Seven Lamps of Architecture,*[29] and this one remark is enough to indicate the nature of the change.

From the height of the mid-century the engaging gingerbread of such structures as Endsleigh had become not so much 'characteristic' as artificial; and a house of this kind seemed now to be not so much a house as the spurious biography of one, scarcely so much a building as a building transposed according to the necessities of theater.

**A very unaffected parsonage is building by Mr. Butterfield at Coalpit Heath, near Bristol. We think he has succeeded in giving the peculiar character required for such a building.**

It is again *The Ecclesiologist,*[30] and St. Saviour's Vicarage, Coalpit Heath (Plate 30) might well stand as an almost perfect exemplification of the new interpretation.

Obviously it had come to be felt that, as so far expressed, character had been an affair of the surface only, that the Picturesque had played with 'the characteristic' as an idea rather than it had respected character as 'a fact.' Picturesque eclecticism was now seen to have detached the externals of every style from the particular conditions of which they were the physical embodiment, and then arbitrarily to have infused these externals with a universal and an apparently self-generated spirit, by appeal to which, though all styles had been provided with a means of resurrection, they had also been condemned to an afterlife as backdrops to an unchanging psychological constant. And if this constant, character, unconditioned by systems of ideas, casually enjoying a haphazard relationship with history, using its styles merely as a variable decor, had now come to appear an unjustifiable impersonation, so the history which it presumed seemed an endless charade, an irrelevant display, where constantly changing scenery and costumes, agreeably agitating the spectators, might provide the actors with pleasing opportunity for the display of their unchanging selves but could otherwise have no relationship to the performance.

The architects of the mid-century, and not only the Gothic Revivalists, revolting against these further implications of the Picturesque, seemed to have sensed that character can hardly initiate itself, and that personality is not extraneous to a specific culture but partly its result. Thus, while they still saw character as a pre-eminently 'natural' quality, they no longer accepted it to be the mark of some 'natural' man, untrameled by society and freely operating in a cultural vacuum. Instead they came to envisage it as the product of specific circumstances, as the vindicating evidence of a genuine interaction between a given individual, given material conditions, and a given cultural milieu. Character became now a quality to be extracted. It was implicit in the limiting data of the problem, from them it was to be educed and through them revealed; so that as the former idea of 'the characteristic' receded, there emerged a new and 'real' conception of character as a form of exposure or revelation.

So much is obvious; but this mid-century conception consistently eludes adequate summary. Contemporaries experienced it, expressed it, but were scarcely able to reduce it to words. Perhaps it was most completely illuminated by *The Seven Lamps of Architecture*; but possibly it was most succinctly defined by Horatio Greenough:

When I define Beauty as the promise of Function; Action as the presence of Function; Character as the record of Function; I arbitrarily divide that which is essentially one. I consider the phases through which organised intention passes to completeness as if they were distinct entities. Beauty being the promise of function, must be mainly present before the phase of action; but so long as there is yet a promise of function there is beauty, proportioned to its relationship with action or character. There is somewhat of character at the close of the first epoch of the organic life, as there is somewhat of beauty at the commencement of the last, but they are less apparent and present rather to the reason than to sensuous tests.

If the normal development of organised life be from beauty to action, from action to character, the progress is a progress upward as well as forward; and action will be higher than beauty even than the summer is higher than the spring; and character will be higher than action, even as the autumn is the resume and the result of spring and summer. If this be true, the attempt to prolong the phase of beauty into the epoch of action can only be made through non-performance; and false beauty or embellishment will be the result.[31]

In these two paragraphs Greenough condenses much, though not all, that was implicit in the less stringently analytical criticism of his day; and from them it may be sensed how character which, in the first case, had been appreciated as a subjective and empirical value, was now transposed as an objective and transcendental one; and how—at the most abstracted level—it could further be understood as the eminently moral resolution of the dialectic between being and becoming, of a conflict between 'beauty' and 'action.'

The idea was elevated, the practice contorted; and, in fact, the intensified evaluation of character now simply brought on that brutalizing of the Picturesque which might be considered the central crisis of the charade. For, since it was now "non-performance" to "attempt to prolong the phase of beauty into the epoch of action," and since the 'promising' condition "beauty" was now organically predestined to suffer transformation through the workings of the "higher" quality character, it was essential that it should bear the scars of the ordeal. Thus, although it has rarely been associated with such buildings as St. Saviour's Vicarage, the American sculptor's reasoning provides almost perfect explanation of this house and of all those other buildings of the mid-century in which the distinction between the characteristic and the visually pleasing has been forced out *en clair*, buildings where character has ceased to be a lyrical adjunct to a pictorial composition and has now been erected as an inexorable absolute which need not beguile but which might outrage. And, if at St. Saviour's Vicarage, Endsleigh, and all other *cottages ornés* have been made 'real,' this same reappraisal of character as an almost mystical "record of Function" could obviously be illustrated just as adequately by the American equivalents of these English buildings.

The parallel would not of course be exact, since by English standards the Picturesque is a retarded movement in the United States, while in America, except in certain Anglophile circles, the Gothic Revival is largely without Tractarian nuances. But, in addition, since structural techniques are dissimilar there is a further distance which must be observed; but, after allowing for some chronological variation and further distinctions of content and medium, such a house as Kingscote in Newport, R.I. (Plate 31), still could reasonably be allowed to represent Ends-leigh, while Richard Morris Hunt's Griswold House, also in Newport (Plate 32), might provide a complement to St. Saviour's Vicarage. And if the charms of the first are less enticing than those of its English equivalent, the 'realism' of the second is scarcely any less ambivalent.

For in seeking to make of character a specific value the architects of the mid-century had been led to a very complicated knotting together of commitments. The demand for characteristic expression had been a corollary of the Romantic consciousness of nature and history, of freedom and individuality. But a less ecstatic approach to nature and a more sophisticated historical culture, with a recognition that freedom predicated necessity, and individuality society, had resulted in a much more closed and highly charged situation. "If he is in earnest his work will not be deficient in character," *The Ecclesiologist*[32] says of the architect. But, if it was now impossible to be in earnest about the Picturesque—because it was wholly empirical, because it required taste rather than faith from its adherents—what contemporary alternative was there? Apparently there was none. Picturesque ideals had penetrated the last strongholds of the academic tradition. The fundamental question was therefore one of limiting the Picturesque, of authenticating it by an increased cultivation of its twin bases in 'nature' and 'history,' that is, of making the Picturesque objective by implicating it with function and techniques, of making it legitimate by restricting its expression to one style. And thus, paradoxically, from the demand for 'reality' there resulted a simultaneous commitment to a structural ideal and to an archeological one.

It is possibly from the force of this antithesis that much architecture of the mid-nineteenth century acquires its distinctive hardness and ferocity. Character as intrinsic to technique and performance was not to be detached from the cognate idea of character as intrinsic to style. The two ideas were interactive; and thus, while the one, by requiring the exhibition of qualities inherent in the substance of building, generated a tradition which has been continuous, it did so, at least partly, by means of an emotional substructure provided by the other.

The High Victorian interpretation of character has had a long and distinguished progeny; but the degree of tension implicit in its formulation of ethical rationalism, its intellectual austerity, its compulsive but not convincing logic, made it too strenuous a system to be long sustained and by the seventies a new situation had arisen.

As explanation of the spectacle of the so-called Queen Anne Revival and as a commentary on the failure of the Gothic, an anonymous critic was quoted at length in *Building News* for January 16, 1874:

In certain aspects the Gothic Revival may be aptly compared with the pre-Raphaelite movement in painting. Both were profoundly in earnest, and in both the rejection of certain qualities of artistic attractiveness ultimately led to a protest from within their own body. The dominant motive in the Gothic Revival was constructive. It sought eagerly to reveal the rudimentary impulses in building, and devoted its energies into carrying into view the structural facts which are actually important. The pre-Raphaelite movement showed an equal worship of naturalism. Everything was to be true and natural and nothing was to be composed. Indeed it may be said that the revolution in both arts involved a neglect of composition, and as a consequence, both revolutions failed in giving to their less imaginative efforts those lighter graces which composition alone can supply. It is a desire for the lighter graces of composition that lies at the root of the new love for the style of Queen Anne. . . .[33]

Contemporary criticism of the Gothic Revival was rarely upon this level; but, in general, observers made the same point which is summarized by a correspondent of the *American Architect and Building News* who signs himself 'Georgian': people did Queen Anne because they liked it, and "after all this is not a very bad reason."[34]

Thirty—even ten—years earlier, it would have seemed one of the worst of all possible reasons, but in the more relaxed atmosphere of the seventies the doctrinaire commitments of the mid-century were no longer to be tolerated; "the lighter graces of composition" could once more be exercised without sense of shame; and, while a patronage of Gothic Revival principles persisted, they were no longer generally received as sanctioned by dogma. They were regarded rather as principles which, according to the architect's tact, might, but need not necessarily, be adhered to. Thus in much the same way that academic theory had continued, as a type of survival doctrine enjoying a sentimental rather than an active endorsement, so Gothic Revival ideas persisted into this neo-Picturesque phase.

Not unexpectedly, after the rigorous demands of the mid-century, in both theory and practice there was now a conspicuous slackening of creative nerve, and over a period of years there was something of a hiatus in the production of significant criticism. It might be said that these ensuing years are marked by a sense of drift, by a general agreement to doubt the mid-century theoretical structure, but by no particular willingness to demolish it; and it might also be observed that neither the mundane scepticism nor the aesthetic languor which came progressively to dominate the period were exactly propitious for the inspiration of any new critical synthesis. It is symptomatic of the new spirit that even the historian of the

Gothic Revival should find himself exposed to the cogency of its empirical judgments, since Eastlake, as the final test of a good building, proposes the question which some years earlier might have seemed the supreme impertinence—"Is it offensive to the eye?"[35] Presumably this question was frequently asked, and as, by the exercise of a simple pragmatism, the Gothic Revival came to be judged and found wanting, so architects were enabled to celebrate their new feelings for textural effects, for increased light, for sparkling detail, for formal equalities admitting no other regulation than that of individual taste.

This sudden disengagement from a High Victorian 'reality' now conceived as being profoundly unrealistic is merely one indication of that general movement towards an art of pure form which typifies the later nineteenth century. The opposed demands of style and structure had been proved too great, their antithesis had been discovered an irrelevance, and the new satisfaction with the visual image as adequate in itself had promoted a distinctly less exacting ideal which acted to dissolve both archeological and structural demands. Obviously historical reminiscence did not cease, but convictions as to its ultimate significance became progressively modified; and no longer preoccupied with 'truth' as required by the Gothic Revivalists, but rather with 'effect' as understood by the Picturesque, architects were again led to recognize frankly compositional disciplines.

But if it could now be asserted that attractive visual appearance was enough, it was still equally mandatory that appropriate character should be displayed—and the contradiction was apparently not a source of embarrassment. Character was by now imbued with an irresistible emotional potency, and although its High Victorian dignity appears as insidiously devalued, the demand for characteristic expression continued unabated. From the seventies onward it is evident that the ascription of character to a building is an act of unchallengeable praise, and Eastlake for instance writes of a certain church that

the Picturesque grouping of the aisle windows, the rich inlay and carving of the reredos . . . even the iron work of the screen, are all full of character, and that type of character which if verbally expressed could only be a synonym for artistic grace.[36]

Clearly character is no longer the new and poetical architectural attribute which it had been for the Picturesque, nor is it the objective architectural condition arrived at by an unyielding and energetic analysis which it was for the midcentury. It is now a luscious psychological accessory of composition whose necessary presence it is assumed that no critic will deny.

In such terms one might distinguish the manors of Norman Shaw—of a compositional brilliance before unknown—from the mid-century achievements of a Butterfield or a Teulon. In mid-century terms the achievement of Norman Shaw is irresponsible, sentimental, and shameless. In Shavian terms the works of the mid-century are defiant of composition and express their defiance in the form of deliberate clumsiness, excessive vigor, and superfluous brutality; for unlike the Gothic Revival, Norman Shaw's is an essentially 'compositional' architecture, and in such a house as Grimsdyke at Harrow Weald (1872; Plate 33) he reasserted the compositional ideals of the Picturesque with an unsparing virtuosity.

Compared with any house of the mid-century, Grimsdyke is immediately satisfying to the eye. Where a house of ten years earlier, Bestwood Lodge for instance (Plate 34), shocks, Grimsdyke soothes; and where Bestwood Lodge is strident, Grimsdyke is ingratiating. At Grimsdyke, unrelated to any systematic scheme of thought, by now quite divested of ideally Romantic overtones, displaying a more complicated and synthetic, a more brilliant and cloying orchestration, at once sentimental and surreptitious, character is exhibited with an assurance and a weightiness which were before unknown. Where once it had been edifying, it is now seductive; and where once it had been 'real,' it is now unabashed.

It may be felt that the idea of character, almost like the Romantic conception of individualism, had passed its creative zenith in the fifties and sixties, and that, as the century wore on, the demand was no longer such as could initiate further significant developments. In fact, as the ideological excitement of the Gothic Revival receded into the past, as High Victorian activity came to be found increasingly intemperate, and as the *laissez-faire* empiricism of the seventies (so well represented by the earlier Norman Shaw) came to appear excessive, so the expression of character came to be increasingly codified and restricted.

A matter of sixteen years separates Norman Shaw's Grimsdyke from his 170 Queen's Gate (Plate 35); their American equivalents, Richardson's Watts Sherman House (1874; Plate 36) and McKim's H. A. C. Taylor House (Plate 37), are separated by only eleven; but during these years, as the 'propriety' of these later houses shows, the extreme characterization which the Gothic Revival had demanded had become unacceptable. A new urbanity had emerged and character was already restricted to that 'correct' character, which it is permissible, which it is indeed necessary that a gentleman should display; while if there was no gentleman who would yet assail directly the mid-century critical canon there were many who now felt obliged to propose some alternative.

Surprisingly John Root in Chicago was one of these, demanding that truth, sincerity, reticence, modesty, etc., the distinguishing marks of the gentleman, should

also be recognized as the marks of excellence in building[37]—a thesis which, with
the very slightest modifications, has persisted down to our own day and which
was perhaps most aptly summarized by John Belcher's *Essentials in Architecture*
(1907). The architectural qualities which Belcher recognizes as 'essential,'—
Strength, Vitality, Restraint, Refinement, Repose, Grace, Breadth, Scale, are very
much an index to the feelings of the time, while their mere enumeration is sufficient to suggest how tempered by taste the violent individualism of the mid-nineteenth century had become by the early years of the twentieth. Character, it may
be suggested, had at last been translated as the outward sign of judicious behavior;
and, just as the gentleman will signalize a specific activity by a change of clothing,
so it seems to have been hoped the building would defer to the conventional
wardrobe by which its purpose might most appropriately be expressed.

And, as both 170 Queen's Gate and the H. A. C. Taylor House illustrate, this
transformation of the 'natural' man of the first years of the century into the responsible gentleman of the last was not without its effects on the organization of
the building. Both houses of course are extreme and precocious examples of a
general tendency, and the final critical attitude which they predicated hardly
emerged with any degree of clarity for some years—scarcely indeed until the publication of Guadet's *Eléments et theorie de l'architecture* inspired a series of
American and British attempts to provide its English equivalent. It is thus that
from approximately the year 1900 onward there followed that succession of
treatises, the composition books, which prompted this investigation. They were a
means by which it was hoped that certain nineteenth century problems might
finally be put to rest.

"Composition," Frank Lloyd Wright tells us, "is dead"; and although this seems
doubtful, if it is indeed the case, it would surely be injudicious to probe into the
precise circumstances of so recent a demise. It might rather be suggested that at
some time in the 1920s the central tenet of the composition books, that architecture has at all times and in all places been determined by the interaction of composition and character, came to seem as improbable as it did in the mid-nineteenth century; and that at the same time the claim of early twentieth century
architectural theory to reveal the underlying and permanent attributes of architectural experience came to present itself as no more than the rationale of an eclectic
situation.

**Composition is the keynote of architectural design. Whilst primarily the plan of a
building dominates its external expression, yet devoid of a sense of "Composi-**

tion" the external effect may be dull and uninteresting despite a good plan; and with a proper appreciation of contrasts and values the same work may be masterly. Detail is secondary, and may be bad or entirely omitted, on a building the mass of which is effective and even spectacular.[38]

Difficult though it sometimes is to disagree with pronouncements of this order, it might be guessed that it was against what seemed to be their unduly self-assured tone that architects like Wright revolted. For where the mid-nineteenth century reaction against the Picturesque had attempted to achieve some kind of synthesis between the laws of structure, the nature of materials, and the intimate and objective qualities of style, the late nineteenth and early twentieth century reaction was led almost exclusively to emphasize phenomena of vision; and, by using history as a kind of dictionary, to deduce from it certain formal schemes apparently quite extrinsic to any particular style or culture. In fact, by detaching the irrational element style from the recently abstracted principles of composition, the dominant theory of the early twentieth century to some extent recapitulated at a more refined and sophisticated level the situation of c. 1830; while as a corollary, the later protest against this eclectic theory very curiously paralleled the earlier protest of the mid-nineteenth century.

But composition can scarcely have suffered so drastic a fate as character, which now can only appear as the leitmotif of an era gone beyond recall. An architecture which aspires to abstraction, which professes a demand for anonymity, which seeks "what is typical, the norm, not the accidental but the definite ad hoc form"[39] can scarcely require the display of character; while the preference for impersonal, neutral, standardized solutions is equally incompatible with the idea of characteristic expression.

According to N. C. Curtis (one of the most distinguished of the eclectic theorists): "the architecture of antiquity was not strongly characterised. The Greeks were not under any necessity for distinguishing between the different types of building by accentuating their character."[40] According to Guadet:: *"La recherche du caractère est d'ailleurs une conception relativement moderne. L'antiquité a bien des édifices nettement caractérisés, mais elle ne paraît cependant avoir fait du caractère un mérite capitale."*[41] But if it must be doubted whether modern architecture any more than that of antiquity entertains a problem of character, it should be recognized that in the problems which character initiated, problems which for the nineteenth century were insoluble ones, there are to be found origins of some of the more significant attitudes by which the present day is distinguished.

Perhaps at no time other than the late eighteenth century has architectural thought been confronted with so explosive an idea; and certainly no other architectural explosion can have created so portentous a vacuum. Limitless experiment was justified by the emergency, the wildest nonconformity flourished exotically among the debris. New experiences were stimulated by the chaos, new energies released by the confusion; both by arbitrary choice and pressure of circumstances, new conceptions of form were generated. By the demand for character, order was atomized. It was reduced to *characteristic* particles; and not until this requirement was dissipated could any effective synthesis of these be envisaged. As a projection of these circumstances the critical embargo upon the term becomes comprehensible. It is an idea which, by emphasizing the particular, the personal, and the curious, will always vitiate system; and it is, perhaps, the fundamental demand which typifies the architecture of the nineteenth century.

## Notes

1 The following is a probably incomplete list of these books: J. V. Van Pelt, *Discussion of Composition*, New York, 1902; J. B. Robinson, *Architectural Composition*, New York, 1908; N. C. Curtis, *Architectural Composition*, New York, 1923; D. Varon, *Architectural Composition*, New York, 1923; H. Robertson, *Principles of Architectural Composition*, London, 1924; and related to these, but not using the word composition in their titles, there might also be cited: J. F. Harbeson, *Study of Architectural Design*, New York, 1922; and E. Pickering, *Architectural Design*, New York, 1933. But other publications of similar content will no doubt suggest themselves.

2 Philip Johnson, *Mies van der Rohe*, New York, 1947, p. 184.

3 Frank Lloyd Wright, *Modern Architecture*, Princeton, N.J., 1931. This statement forms a repeating pattern all over the end papers of the book. I have been unable to locate it in the text.

4 John Ruskin, *Stones of Venice*, London, 1850, Vol. II, Ch. VI, paragraph 42: "I am always afraid to use this word 'Composi-

tion'; it is so utterly misused in the general parlance respecting art. Nothing is more common than to hear divisions of art into 'form, composition and colour,' or 'light and shade and composition,' or it matters not what else and composition, the speakers in each case attaching a perfectly different meaning to the word, generally an indistinct one, and always a wrong one. Composition is, in plain English, 'putting together' . . ."

5 Pickering, p. 278.

6 Robert Morris, *Lectures on Architecture*, London, 1734, pp. 67-68.

7 Robert Adam, *Works in Architecture* . . . , London, 1778, Preface.

8 Sir Joshua Reynolds, *Literary Works*, London, 1835, Vol. II, p. 76. From Discourse III delivered in 1786.

9 William Atkinson, *Views of Picturesque Cottages*, London, 1805; Robert Lugar, *Architectural Sketches for Rural Dwellings*, London, 1805; C. A. Busby, *A series of designs for villas and country houses*, London, 1808; Edmund Aikin, *Designs for Villas and Other Rural Dwellings*, London, 1810; J. B. Papworth, *Rural Residences*, London, 1818;

P. F. Robinson, *Rural Architecture*, London, 1833; P. F. Robinson, *Designs for Ornamental Villas*, London, 1836. A number of these books are without pagination and their texts are for the most part so liberally scattered with the new terminology that no specific references have been given for the quotations which follow.

10 Emil Kaufmann, *Architecture in the Age of Reason*, Cambridge, Mass., 1955, pp. 130-31.

11 J. C. Loudon, *The Landscape Gardening and Landscape Architecture of the Late Humphrey Repton, Esq.*, London, 1840, pp. 130-131.

12 J. B. Papworth, *Ornamental Gardening*, London, 1818.

13 J. B. Papworth, *Rural Residences*, London, 1818, p. 45.

14 J. C. Loudon, "The Principles of Criticism in Architecture," *Encyclopedia of Cottage, Farm and Villa Architecture*, London, 1833, p. 1120.

15 Reynolds, Vol. I, p. 333. From Discourse III delivered in 1770.

16 The sentiment is expressed in Goethe's *Von Deutsche Baukunst*, 1770-73.

17 Sir John Soane, *Lectures on Architecture*, Arthur T. Bolton, ed., London, 1929, p. 178. From Lecture XI, apparently read for the first time in 1815.

18 A. J. Downing, *Cottage Residences*, New York, 1873, pp. 12-13.

19 "Mr Petit's Remarks on Church Architecture," *The Ecclesiologist*, Vol. I, 1842, p. 87.

20 G. E. Street, "On the Revival of the Ancient Style of Domestic Architecture," *The Ecclesiologist*, Vol. XIV, 1853, p. 70.

21 "Mr Petit's Ecclesiological Position," *The Ecclesiologist*, Vol. VI, 1846, p. 129.

22 C. R. Cockerell, "Royal Academy Lectures," *Atheneum*, London, 1843.

23 *The Ecclesiologist*, Vol. VI.

24 *Ibid.*, Vol. XII, 1851, p. 241.

25 *Ibid.*, Vol. XIV.

26 G. E. Street, *Brick and Marble Architecture in the Middle Ages*, London, 1855, p. 109.

27 *The Ecclesiologist*, Vol. I, 1842, p. 94.

28 Unknown source.

29 John Ruskin, *The Seven Lamps of Architecture*, London, 1849, p. 45.

30 *The Ecclesiologist*, Vol. VI.

31 Henry T. Tuckerman, *A Memorial of Horatio Greenough*, New York, 1853, p. 133. From an essay by Greenough, "Relative and Independent Beauty."

32 *The Ecclesiologist*, Vol. VI.

33 *Building News*, Vol. XXVI, January 16, 1874. It is interesting to notice that precisely this criticism of the architects of the mid-century was later to be made in France. See J. Guadet, *Eléments et Théorie de l'Architecture*, Paris, 1902, Vol. I, p. 108: "Henri Labrouste enseignait: L' Architecture est l'art de bâtir. C'était une définition de combat, une protestation contre le dédain trop réel de la construction chez certaines écoles d' alors. Mais cette définition, pour être plus incisif, était incomplète et pêchait à son tour par l' oubli de la composition artistique."

34 *American Architect and Building News*, Vol. II, October 20, 1877.

35 C. L. Eastlake, *The Gothic Revival*, London, 1872, p. 333.

36 *Ibid.*, p. 324.

37 Harriet Monroe, *John Root*, New York,
1896, p. 77 and *passim*. From a paper read
before the Chicago Architectural Sketch
Club and published in *The Inland Architect.*

38 H. Robertson, *Principles of Architectural
Composition*, London, 1924, Preface.

39 Peter Blake, *Marcel Breuer*, New York,
1949, p. 129.

40 Curtis, pp. 3-4.

41 Guadet, Vol. I, p. 133.

Plate 28   Woolley Park, Berkshire. Jeffry
Wyatt, 1799.

Plate 29   Endsleigh, Devonshire. Jeffry
Wyatt, 1810.

Plate 30   St. Saviour's Vicarage, Coalpit
Heath. William Butterfield, 1845.

Plate 31   Kingscote, Newport, R.I. Richard Upjohn, 1841.

Plate 32   J. N. A. Griswold House, Newport, R.I. Richard Morris Hunt, 1862-3.

Plate 33   Grimsdyke, Harrow Weald. Richard
Norman Shaw, 1872.

Plate 34   Bestwood Lodge, Nottinghamshire.
Samuel Sanders Teulon, 1862.

Plate 35   170 Queen's Gate, London. Richard
Norman Shaw, 1888.

Plate 36   Watts Sherman House, Newport,
R.I. H. H. Richardson and Stanford White,
1874.

Plate 37   H. A. C. Taylor House, Newport,
R.I. McKim, Mead and White, 1886.

# Chicago Frame

First published in the *Architectural Review*,
1956.

The skeleton of the steel or concrete frame is almost certainly the most recurrent motif in contemporary architecture, and is surely among the most ubiquitous of what Siegfried Giedion would have designated its *constituent elements.* Perhaps the role of the frame is most aptly summarized in the drawing by which Le Corbusier illustrated the structural system of his experimental Domino House (Plate 12), but, while its primary function is evident, apart from this practical value, the frame has obviously acquired a significance which is less recognized.

Apparently the neutral grid of space which is enclosed by the skeleton structure supplies us with some particularly cogent and convincing symbol, and for this reason the frame has established relationships, defined a discipline, and generated form. The frame has been the catalyst of an architecture; but one might notice that the frame has also *become* architecture, that contemporary architecture is almost inconceivable in its absence. Thus, one recalls innumerable buildings where the frame puts in an appearance even when not structurally necessary; one has seen buildings where the frame appears to be present when it is not; and, since the frame seems to have acquired a value quite beyond itself, one is often prepared to accept these aberrations. For, without stretching the analogy too far, it might be fair to say that the frame has come to possess a value for contemporary architecture equivalent to that of the column for classical antiquity and the Renaissance. Like the column, the frame establishes throughout the building a common ratio to which all the parts are related; and, like the vaulting bay in the Gothic cathedral, it prescribes a system to which all parts are subordinate.

It is the universality of the frame and the ease with which it has apparently directed our plastic judgment which has led to the focusing of so much attention upon the Chicago commercial architecture of the eighties and early nineties (Plate 38). In Chicago, seemingly, our own interests were so directly anticipated that if—as we apparently sometimes conceive it to be—the frame structure is the essence of modern architecture, then we can only assume a relationship between ourselves and Chicago comparable to that of the High Renaissance architects with Florence, or of the High Gothic architects to the Ile-de-France. For, although the steel frame did make occasional undisguised appearances elsewhere, it was in Chicago that its formal results were most rapidly elucidated.

For some ten years the architects of Chicago devoted themselves to the solution of typical problems of the frame; and, before the end of this time, they had achieved results which are still today unsurpassed for their elegance and economy. But, admiring these results and acknowledging this great achievement, one is still disposed to ask of these Chicago buildings whether they are indeed representatives

of a 'modern' architecture. Certainly the process of their design was as rational
and as direct as that of any modern building is supposed to be. Certainly these
buildings are lacking in both rhetoric and sentimental excess; but, also, there is
about them a quality of rudimentary magnificence, a flavor at once more heroic
and more brutal than is to be found in any building of the present day. These
structures make no compromise with the observer; they are neither capricious nor
urbane and they display an authenticity so complete that we are disposed to accept them as facts of nature, as geological manifestations rather than as architectural achievements. "In Chicago," says Louis Sullivan, "the tall building would
seem to have arisen spontaneously in response to favourable physical conditions
. . . The Future looked bright. The flag was in the breeze. . . ."[1] In Chicago we are
led to believe that the slate was at last wiped clean, the break with 'the styles' was
made, and the route of future development defined.

The alleged debacle which overwhelmed these Chicago architects of the eighties
is common knowledge. The World Columbian Exhibition cut short their development; public taste no longer endorsed their decisions; and, although for some few
their principles remained luminous, it was not until comparatively recently that
their figures reemerged, sanctified and established in the Pantheon of architectural
progress.

But the disaster was never quite so complete as our sense of myth requires that
it should have been; and, as we know, pockets of resistance survived which eclecticism could not obliterate, so that it was again in Chicago that a second and
equally decisive contribution to present-day architecture was made. Montgomery
Schuyler, one of the most devoted apologists of the Chicago School, writing of
the city in the nineties, noticed that its architectural expressions were twofold
only—"places of business and places of residence." The image of Chicago which
remained in the mind he found to be "the sum of innumerable impressions made
up exclusively of the skyscraper of the city and the dwellings of the suburbs. Not
a church enters into it," he says, "Scarcely a public building enters into it . . .
Chicago has no more a Nouvel Opéra than it has a Notre Dame."[2] It was a relatively uncomplicated situation which Schuyler recognized, a situation dominated
by two building types—the commercial structures of the Loop and their suburban
complement. And, with the nineties, the spirit of experiment may be said simply
to have transferred itself from one of these types to the other, so that it became
in Oak Park that Frank Lloyd Wright was to conduct those researches into architectural form whose results now seem to have been preeminently superior to any
other achievement of that day. The much publicized contributions of van de

Velde, of Horta, Olbrich, Hoffmann, Loos, Perret, McKintosh, and Voysey can only appear as irresolute and undirected when compared with the astonishing finality of these early works of Wright's, which, although less implacable than the office buildings of the Loop, are every bit as conclusive. These houses are the monuments of an unerringly consistent development; and to informed observers of the time it was apparent that here a plastic statement of the very highest relevance was in process of delivery, that here a definite answer had already been given to those questions which many of the most advanced buildings of the day seemed to exist merely to propose.

The international impact of this early phase of Wright's career is a matter of history; and, if the exact influence which the publication of his work exerted in Europe may remain a matter of dispute, it can scarcely be denied that in such a building as the Gale House (Plate 39) of 1909 Wright had already defined principles of form which at least very closely parallel those enunciated ten years later by van Doesburg, or by Rietveld in *De Stijl's* major architectural monument, his Schröder House (Plate 40) of 1924. In each case the vision of an architecture as a composition of sliding planes predominates; and Wright's anticipation of this idea seems to have been as complete as Chicago's earlier anticipation of the formal role which the frame structure was destined to play.

This priority of Chicago's contribution need not imply a dependence elsewhere upon it. Obviously both van Doesburg and Rietveld could claim a legitimate descent from the innovations which Cubism had introduced; obviously too, Le Corbusier's preoccupation with problems of the frame structure derives not from the steel skeleton of Chicago but from the reinforced concrete frame of Auguste Perret. But neither of these observations can obscure the apparent evidence that Chicago did seem to experience a prevision of two of the major themes of twentieth century architecture—the frame structure and the composition of intersecting planes.

This apparent insight of Chicago's is widely recognized; but its recognition has created certain acute critical problems. Wright's achievement was scarcely likely to pass into oblivion; but the renewed consciousness of Chicago's earlier contribution which has been stimulated by the later work of Mies van der Rohe is responsible for a conspicuous interpretative embarrassment. Thus, although we know it to be different in kind, we are apt to feel that Mies's campus of the Illinois Institute of Technology is the polished culmination of a rationalism identical with that displayed by Jenney in the Second Leiter Building (Plate 41); but, equally, we are obliged to believe that at least a partial explanation of the intuitive certainty which so early distinguished Wright's work was provided by his own personal relationship with the older masters of the Chicago School. We can understand that his own audaciousness was reinforced by their daring, his own sense of order by theirs, his own precocity by those qualities which have led so many observers to see in the commercial buildings of Chicago the most complete adumbration of contemporary forms.

But it is at this point that the judgment of the present day discovers its dilemma. Although we may assert that the architects of the office buildings in the Loop clarified a basic disposition of twentieth century architecture, yet for the structural skeleton which their achievement exposed, it can only be said that Wright (who might be considered their most illustrious pupil) seems to have shown a most marked distaste.

With the exception of the Larkin Building in Buffalo and the S. C. Johnson Company's Administration Building at Racine, Wright has, of course, built no large office buildings; and it might therefore be claimed that he had no reason to employ the frame structure. But even in the Larkin Building the cathedrallike internal space suggests a certain aversion to those conclusions of the Chicago School whose relevance is so enthusiastically acclaimed today; while in the Johnson Administration Building an entirely different conception of structure is entertained. Admittedly a number of early skyscraper projects—e.g., the Luxfer Prism Skyscraper (Plate 42) and the Lincoln Center—are for steel frame buildings; and, in 1912, the Press Building for San Francisco (Plate 43) shows a concrete frame; but in all of these designs a Sullivanian influence is to be detected, and in none of them are we made aware of that inimitable world of Wrightian form which characterizes the domestic designs of the same years. We can believe that, in all these instances, Wright was struggling with a problem which he felt to be intractable and found to be unsympathetic, and it is not until the National Life Insurance Company Skyscraper project of 1924 (Plate 44) that this problem seems to become clarified and we find the sharp revelation of the differences in outlook which identify Wright's development as something apart from that of his predecessors in Chicago.

The classic Chicago office buildings, like the classic palaces of Renaissance Italy, were conceived as single volumes, or when situation did not permit the appearance of a volume, as single facades. Like Italian palazzi they overwhelm the observer by their economy of motif and consistency of theme; while, as architectural expression, they present no more than an unmodified surface exhibiting a rationally integrated and well-proportioned structure. But Wright's building is distinguished by the observance of quite contrary principles; and, rather than a single structurally articulated block, it displays a highly developed composition of transparent volumes, while rather than the 'static' structural solution of the frame it presents the more 'dynamic' motif of the cantilever which had already been employed in the Imperial Hotel. Thus, while conceptually this building is radically distinct from Chicago's earlier contributions to skyscraper design whose architects had attempted neither such elaboration nor such openness, technically also it is distinct, since both its construction and its curtain wall constitute an innovation in the Chicago tradition.

According to Henry-Russell Hitchcock, "Wright has likened the special construction used in the (Imperial) Hotel to the balance of a tray on a waiter's fingers";[3] and the structural members both in that building and the 1924 project do seem to have been conceived in that way—as a series of nuclei generating around themselves intelligible volumes of space. This preference, already presumed by Wright's old preoccupation with the central chimney stack, must explain some of his reluctance to use a regular skeletal frame which scarcely permits such an interpretation of structure; but the indivisible fusion of structure and space which Wright has designated 'organic' is scarcely realized in either the Tokyo building or the National Life Insurance Company project, and it is not until the St. Mark's Tower scheme of 1929 that it first becomes explicit at a major scale (Figure 7, Plate 45).

The spaces created by the St. Mark's Tower are at last of an unmistakably Wrightian order and, understandably, the tower has been the prototype for all the tall buildings by him which have followed. Aggregations of St. Mark's Towers are the basis for the 1930 apartment house project and again for the Crystal Heights Hotel (Plate 46) design of 1940; while the tower appears in condensed form as the laboratory building at Racine, Wisconsin, before being finally transcribed as the Price Office Building at Bartlesville, Oklahoma.

Conceptually all these structures present the nucleus of a gigantic mushroom column supporting a series of trays which, as shown by the apartment house and hotel projects, is implied to be systematically extensible by approaching column to column until the circumferences of their trays impinge or even overlap. Like the central core of the chimney and the real mushroom columns of the Johnson Administration Building, the idea of the St. Mark's Tower may seem to derive from the 'organic' demand for the integration of space and structure; and, as fulfilling this demand, the building becomes a single, complete, and self-explanatory utterance.

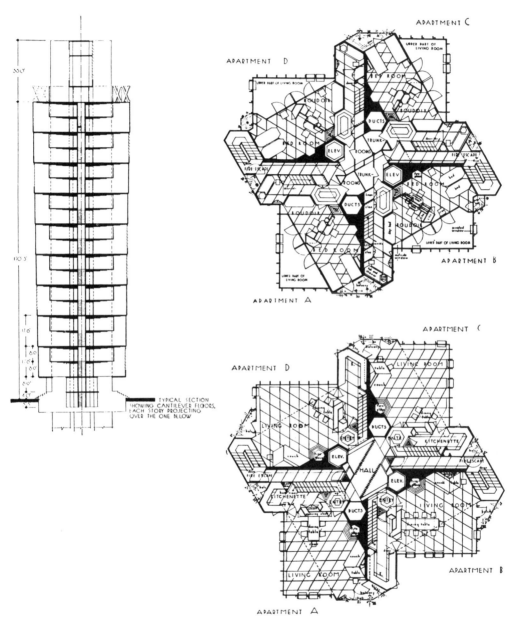

Figure 7    Project, St. Mark's Tower, New
York City. Plan and section. Frank Lloyd
Wright, 1929.

As an extension of the domestic theme the St. Mark's Tower is among Wright's most brilliant and ingenious achievements, and the virtuosity with which it is organized can only arouse the greatest admiration. Its vitality and coherence are undeniable, its plastic control little short of awe-inspiring—admitting the basic premises upon which its inspiration depends, the tower is a superbly logical development; but for very many observers both it and its derivatives can only stand as a series of enlarged question marks. Admiring it as an individual achievement, recognizing it as a highly suggestive exception, these observers are still disposed to ask whether after all it is not a most elaborate evasion of a normal and standard structural fact. The frame, by so many modern architects, has been received almost as a heaven-sent blessing. Why, one inquires, has it been so distinctly rejected on the part of Wright? Did he consider it a merely adventitious shortcut to unimportant solutions? Did he consider it too great a restriction of a 'creative' freedom? Just why did he remain so very unbeguiled by Chicago's first great architectural discovery?

The question is so pressing that one may be justified in proceeding with speculation, and a number of immediate answers suggest themselves. But the answer that Wright's career has been largely in the field of domestic architecture considers the problem only superficially. The use of the steel or concrete frame in domestic architecture may not be necessary, but many conspicuous monuments of the modern movement survive to prove it not abnormal. The answer that America had already discovered an alternative structure in the balloon frame is more convincing, but not completely so. Economy in America recommended the balloon frame, but in Europe economy equally recommended a brick or masonry structure, and by the more significant innovators economy's recommendations were frequently disregarded.

A partial answer has already been suggested in the notice of Wright's highly developed and individual demand for 'organic' space, and here one of the most obvious differences between him and his predecessors in Chicago may be found. Louis Sullivan, for instance, was by no means typical of the Chicago School in general; but a major and unnoticed distinction between Wright and Sullivan, as also between Wright and his other Chicago predecessors, may be found in their feeling for the plan.

For Wright, as for Le Corbusier, the plan has always been a generator of form; and, if the plans of his earliest buildings are in no way remarkable, already in the Blossom House of 1892 (Figure 8) it is quite clear that a disciplined orchestration of spaces had become one of his primary interests, while almost any of his houses

Figure 8   Blossom House, Chicago. Plan.
Frank Lloyd Wright, 1892.

of the next thirty years will reveal how intensively this interest was sustained. Wright's *partis* develop without apparent effort. There are few lapses in his plans, few volumes where his basic rhythms are not experienced; and, in all this he is very definitely to be distinguished from Sullivan, whose most ardent admirers have never claimed for him any highly developed interest in the formal possibilities of the plan. Sullivan's buildings may often be superb assertions of the primacy of structure, but one finds it hard to believe that for him the significance of their plans was other than a negative one. The plans of the Wainwright and Schiller Buildings, for instance, are hardly those of a master, while such a plan as that of the National Farmer's Bank at Owatonna, Minnesota, will scarcely bear analysis.

Sullivan was not primarily a planner. Indeed there was little in his practice which could prompt him to any sophisticated evaluation of the plan. Sullivan was primarily an architect of commercial buildings; and, of all buildings, the office block is obviously that without the need of any but the minimum of planning. It requires elementary circulations and a well lit floor area; but apart from these, it neither can nor should present any spatial elaboration. Thus, the unobstructed evenly lit floor and the indefinite number of floors which it permitted, recommended the steel frame to the architects of Chicago as the answer to a practical dilemma; but also, by the nature of the context in which they explored it, they were necessarily inhibited in the exploration of its spatial possibilities.

With a lack of stylistic prejudice and with a discretion which seem remarkable to us today, the Chicago architects projected on to their facades the neutral structure which they felt to be the reality of the frame behind; and if, as was the case with Sullivan's Wainwright Building in St. Louis and his Guaranty Building in Buffalo, it was considered aesthetically desirable that the frame should be modified, this process was rationalized in terms of the need for psychological expressiveness in the facade rather than in any need for internal spatial excitement.

With little occasion to use the frame for any other program than that of the office building, it is not surprising that the Chicago architects remained unaware of certain of its attributes, so that some explanation of Wright's unwillingness to employ it may possibly be found here. To repeat: unlike Sullivan, who had approached architecture primarily with the object of realizing an expressive structure, Wright was from the first abnormally sensitive to the demands of an expressive space. These demands (one might surmise) he was *compelled* to satisfy, and it was only later (one might believe) that his Sullivanian training reasserted itself to demand a rationalization of this spatial achievement in terms of a generating structure. The monumental construction of the Hillside Home School suggests that a rationalization of this kind was already under way around 1902; and, by 1904, in the Martin House (Figure 9), this process had taken on unmistakable definition. But by then, and supposing Wright to have wished a predominantly structural rationale, his space compositions were already of a richness which would scarcely permit their accommodation within any system so austere as that provided by the Chicago frame.

However, an answer along these lines, suggesting that a cause for Wright's rejection of the frame may be discovered exclusively in the nature of his formal will, can at best provide only a partial explanation of the problem, and a further reason must be offered which may, perhaps, be found to lie in the varieties of significance with which the frame has been endowed.

At the present day, Chicago's failure to arrive at any statement of the frame as a vehicle of spatial expression—when we think about it—seems to be curious. We are now completely accustomed to regard the skeleton structure as a spatial instrument of some power, since it is—after all—some considerable time ago that a formula was evolved permitting the simultaneous appearance of both structural grid and considerable spatial complexity; and most of modern architecture, the so-called International Style, may be said to have been dependent on this formula.

But, in order to arrive at an equation of the demands of space and structure, Le Corbusier and Mies van der Rohe had been led to postulate their functional independence, i.e., the independence of partitions from columns, so that unlike Wright's development—which may be said to proceed from a conviction as to the 'organic' unity of space and structure—the International Style may be seen to issue from an assumption of the separate existence of both according to distinct laws. Wright's structure creates space or is created by it; but in the International Style an autonomous structure perforates a freely abstracted space, acting as its punctuation rather than its defining form. There is thus in the International Style no fusion of space and structure, but each in the end remains an identifiable component, and architecture is conceived, not as their confluence, but rather as their dialectical opposition, as a species of debate between them.

That a solution in these terms was possible for European innovators of the twenties derives, among other reasons, from a particular concept of the frame which they entertained; that such a concept was neither possible, nor to be envisaged, in Chicago of the nineties must be partly explained by a different significance which was there attributed to the skeleton structure. In Chicago it might be said that the frame was convincing as fact rather than as idea, whereas in consider-

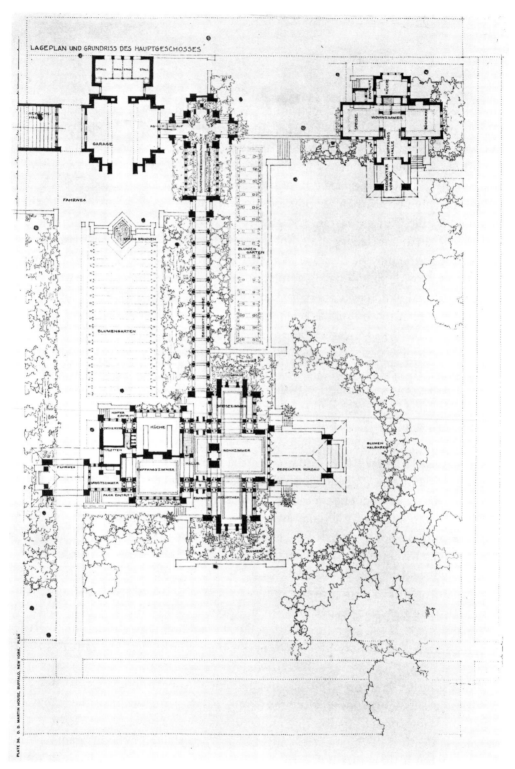

Figure 9   Martin House, Buffalo. Plan.
Frank Lloyd Wright, 1904.

ing the European innovators of the twenties one cannot suppress the supposition that the frame to them was much more often an essential idea before it was an altogether reasonable fact.

In order to clarify these too general observations a classic Chicago building, Holabird and Roche's McGlurg Building of 1899-1900 (Plate 47), might be paralleled with an almost contemporary European building of 1897, Horta's Maison du Peuple in Brussels (Plate 48)—both of them, though different in function, comparable as advanced buildings of their day. Both of them show preoccupation with problems of the frame; but it is the contrast between the rather quiet elegance of the first and the frenetic restlessness of the second which is immediately apparent. The McGlurg Building is a subtle and uncomplicated statement. The Maison du Peuple is an oblique and a highly involved reference. In the McGlurg Building it is possible to suppose that certain practical requirements have been accommodated; in the Maison du Peuple it is impossible not to deduce that certain theoretical desiderata have been stated. In the first, the steel frame presents itself as the solution of a specific problem; while, in the second, *a cast iron prevision of the steel frame* is exposed apparently as the manifesto of an architectural program. Holabird and Roche's structure is primarily a building; Horta's is predominantly a polemic.

There is little doubt that Horta's building cost the greater aesthetic effort; but there is almost complete certainty that Holabird and Roche's is more generally pleasing to the taste of the present day. Of Holabird and Roche's self-consciousness, however, the McGlurg Building offers no assurance; while of Horta's sophistication the Maison du Peuple is indisputable evidence. In Horta's case one can guess at a hyperawareness of the response his building was likely to evoke. One can sense the anticipation of extended controversy, critical explanations, avant-garde delight, conservative horror. The Maison du Peuple is a building offered to a society; and, whether society will accept or reject it, Horta still assumes its participation as an audience. That is, Horta invites reaction; and, accordingly, the Maison du Peuple exhibits a humanity which the McGlurg Building does not display. For there, rather than any subject for the discussion of a coterie, Holabird and Roche have attempted to provide no more than the rational envelope for the activities of their clients' tenants.

Indeed, if the methods followed by Holabird and Roche at this time were in any way typical of the Chicago School in general, it might safely be assumed that they were definitely not anxious that their building should involve them in any of the excitements of artistic notoriety. In the word of the French novelist, Paul Bourget, whose appreciations of the Chicago School have been constantly quoted, the Chicago architects had "frankly accepted the conditions imposed by the speculator"[4] —they had limited themselves to producing buildings which should be no more than the logical instruments of investment. In other words, being in no position to make manifestos in the cause of rationalism, they were simply obliged—and within the strictest terms—to be as rational as they might.

This distinction between two styles of argument (it is really a question of the idea of mechanization versus the fact), would seem to crystallize the basic differences of approach signified by the two buildings; and it is a distinction which might be extended further. "I asked one of the successful architects of Chicago what would happen if the designer of a commercial building sacrificed the practical availableness of one of its floors to the assumed exigencies of architecture as has often been done in New York," writes Schuyler. "His answer," he continues, "was suggestive. 'Why the word would be passed around and he would never get another one to do. No, we never try tricks on our businessmen, they are too wide awake.' "[5] The businessmen of Chicago, then, were not prepared to make sacrifices for the idea, did not require the overt architectural symbolism which was apparently necessary in New York, did not even require those fantasies upon mechanistic themes which could be obtruded upon the citizens of Brussels; but the Chicago architects (or some of them) were still quite aware that symbolic meaning has ever been among the necessary attributes of architecture; and if, as Schuyler infers, they were compelled to be utilitarian, they were not always unconscious of the social significance of their utilitarianism. John Root, for instance, required that the modern office building should by its "mass and proportion convey in some elemental sense an idea of the great, stable, conserving forces of modern civilization."[6]

But, even in this demand, one might continue to notice a difference between Chicago and Brussels. In Belgium, Siegfried Giedion tells us, it had been discovered that architectural *forms* were impure, that the atmosphere was "infected," and that, in consequence, architectural "progress" was there conceived as a kind of "moral revolt."[7] But the Chicago architects had been scarcely allowed to subject *forms* to so detached a scrutiny; and, had they enjoyed the leisure to do so, if their conclusions had conflicted with the requirements of the speculator, it is to be doubted whether they would have been enabled to put them into practice. "The great, stable, conserving forces of modern civilization" (The great, expanding forces of a *laissez-faire* economic system?) represented for Root a power which it was desirable to express. But for Horta? One must doubt if Horta recognized any such imperative. He, one suspects, had arrived at certain critical conclusions as to the nature of contemporary society and had come then to envisage his work as the architectural manifestation of these judgments.

In Belgium, it is evident, the *art nouveau* was one of those revolutionary movements essentially dependent on a highly developed program; but in Chicago, it should be clear that the structural revolution was largely without any such theoretical support.

"The Chicago activity in erecting high buildings (of solid masonry) finally attracted the attention of the local sales managers of Eastern rolling mills," Sullivan tells us, and it was *they*, he says, who conceived of the idea of a skeleton which would carry the entire weight of the building. From then on, he continues, the evolution of the steel frame "was a matter of vision in salesmanship based upon engineering imagination and technique"; and, in this manner, *as a product for sale*, "the idea of the steel frame was tentatively presented to Chicago architects."

"The passion to sell," Sullivan asserts, "is the impelling power of American life. Manufacturing is subsidiary and adventitious. But selling must be based on a semblance of service—the satisfaction of a need. The need was there, the capacity to satisfy was there, but contact was not there. Then there came the flash of imagination which saw the single thing. The trick was turned and there swiftly came into being something new under the sun."[8]

The Chicago structural revolution therefore was the result of a certain combination: of ruthless open-mindedness and imaginative salesmanship. On Sullivan's admission, the architects of Chicago did not *demand* the frame; it was rather *presented* to them; and this simple fact may explain both the rapid and dispassionate manner in which they contrived to rationalize the frame structure and also the way in which so many of them were able to abandon their method for another and different one. "The architects of Chicago," Sullivan adds, "welcomed the steel frame and did something with it. The architects of the East were appalled by it and could make no contribution to it." But from Schuyler we learn the opposite—that the architects of Chicago were not very different from architects elsewhere. "They are," he writes, "different on compulsion." They have "frankly accepted the conditions imposed by the speculator, because they really are imposed, and there is no getting away from them if one would win and keep the reputation of a 'practical' architect."[9]

Taken together, these two statements are confusing; but they are not perhaps as contradictory as at first they may appear. They describe a situation. They suggest a lack of theoretical awareness. They indicate a responsiveness to the new. They illustrate a willingness to defer to the client. And the clients, Schuyler continues, "the men who project and finance the utilitarian buildings" are not "the most private spirited (but) they are the most public spirited body of businessmen of any commercial city in the world." They are, he says, "the same men who are ready to incur expenditures for public purposes with a generosity and a public spirit that are elsewhere unparalleled." "They are willing to make the most generous sacrifices for their city to provide it with ornaments and trophies which shall make it more than a centre of pig sticking and grain handling. They are willing to play the part of Maecenas to the fine arts, only they insist that they will not play it during business hours."

The candor of these contemporary observations goes a long way to dispose of a critical scheme to which nowadays we pay our respects. It disposes of the dichotomy between the virtuous Chicago of the Loop and the depraved Chicago of the Fair. Magnificently undisguised, the office buildings of the Loop owe something of their authenticity to their being no more than the rationalization of business requirements; but, although they are social documents of the highest importance, in spite of Root's endeavors they are scarcely, in any deliberate and overt sense, cultural symbols. They were conceived as the means to achievement; and, for what was thought to be that achievement itself, it is necessary to look elsewhere, presumably both to the suburban residential development, and to "the ornaments and trophies," the unparalleled expenditures, and "the generous sacrifices," of which those lavished upon the World Columbian exhibition can only appear the most outstanding.

Thus, seen in terms of the admirable pragmatism which actually reared the buildings of the Loop, which was responsible for their directness and lack of gesture, both these and the structures of the Fair, like opposite sides of a coin, come to appear as complementary phenomena. Because business and culture were conceived of as distinct activities, because the commercial magnates of Chicago were not willing "to play the part of Maecenas to the fine arts during business hours," it was possible for the architects of Chicago to proceed with the most audacious innovations; and, because in doing so they offended no expressed social or artistic preference, no check was offered to their remorseless evolution of a basic structural logic. As Schuyler tells us, this rationalization could not have been effected in New York. It could not, as we know, have been effected in Europe. It was possible in Chicago because there *business* was without inhibition; but unhappily, as the World Columbian Exhibition proves, *business* was not for this reason irresponsible.

Thus, what to us appears to have been Chicago's success and Chicago's failure were implicit in the same conditions. A primary architectural achievement was determined by the urgency of a physical need; and, by the lack of a specifically architectural program, an apparently complete architectural revolution was made possible.

But just this lack of program in the end made it not possible for this revolution to become decisive. The office buildings of the Loop were undoubtedly admired by contemporaries; but, however rational their structure and however immaculate their form, it is hard to represent them as the response to any very adequately acceptable notion of society. They invoked no completely receivable public standards; they stipulated only private gain; and for the taste of the time, which had not yet sufficiently expanded—or contracted—to be able to envisage the *machine* with a poetic bias, they were not so much architecture as they were equipment. Stimulating facts they might be; but they were scarcely to be received as facts of culture.

Distinctions such as these which go some way to clarify the other than technical and formal differences between a McGlurg Building and a Maison du Peuple necessarily elicit questions of attitudes and mythologies; and such questions might possibly be brought into sharper focus by the brief analysis of a further pair of buildings which, in *Space, Time and Architecture*, Siegfried Giedion was led to compare: Daniel Burnham's Reliance Building (Plate 49) of 1894 and Mies van der Rohe's Glass Tower project (Plate 50) of 1921.

It is the similarity of these buildings with which Giedion is concerned; and, in terms of a Wölflinian background such as his which tends to ignore problems of content (implying that roughly identical forms suppose roughly approximate meaning), it is the common likeness of the American building and the German project which will command attention. But, if we have here, very obviously, two extensively glazed office towers, it is fundamentally not their similarity but their unlikeness which should most seriously involve us—and particularly so since to emphasize their unlikeness need not involve any great exercise of critical acuity.

Thus, we have a building and a would-be building; the concrete result of a particular problem and the abstract solution of a general one; a building which services an existing requirement and a proposal which relates to a possible future need. We have something which answers and something which anticipates. The Reliance Building rises above the streets of a commercial capital; the Glass Tower soars against a background of wooded hills and above an agglomeration of Gothic roofs; and, if we can scarcely believe the Glass Tower to be a necessity in this toy

city of an older Germany, then also we may know it to be not only the project
for an office building but also the advertisement for a cause. For, if the Reliance
Building, very largely, *is what it is*, the glass tower, like the Maison du Peuple,
very patently, *is something which it does not profess to be*—a highly charged symbolic statement. While the Reliance Building is almost devoid of ideological overtones, the Glass Tower is not only a presumptive building but also an implicit
social criticism.

From these differences of innuendo both building and project derive their weakness and their strength; if the one lacks poetry, the other lacks prose. Burnham,
one might guess, is someone, optimistic about the present, who accepts the prevailing ethos and who envisages the future as its continuance; while Mies, one
could suppose, is someone, not able to collaborate with the existing, who is con-
strained to reject the established and who insists only on the justifications of
time. Which is, of course, grossly to simplify. But, if Burnham's complicity and
Mies's protestation may be equally respectable, they do impose upon their respective products a quite different significance; and, while the Reliance Building remains a direct answer to a technical and functional problem, the Glass Tower, by
inferring an altruistic order of society, continues to be both much less and much
more than this. For, unlike the Reliance Building, the Glass Tower engages both
the moral and the aesthetic interests of our Utopian sentiment.

In Europe in the 1920s it might be said that the tall building such as Mies had
here projected presented itself primarily as a symbol rather than as any object for
use. It was a symbol of a technologically oriented future society and, to a lesser
degree, a symbol of an America which seemed to anticipate that future development; and thus, by circumstances, the idea of the tall building in Europe became
imbued with an ultimate persuasiveness which in America it could not possess. In
Europe the idea of the tall building was apt to be the substance of a dream; but,
in America, the idea become fact was prone to be little more than an aspect of a
too emphatic reality. "The American engineers," writes Le Corbusier, "overwhelm with their calculations our expiring architecture." They are not, he asserts,
"in pursuit of an architectural idea"; rather they are "simply guided by the results
of calculation";[10] and, although this may have been as true of the Chicago architects of the eighties as Le Corbusier felt it to be of the engineers of a later date, it
is only too obvious that the skyscrapers of the ville radieuse are *not* the results of
any comparable calculation. Rather they betray a mind preoccupied with the
ideal order of things. They exude what Dr. Johnson described as "the grandeur of
generality." They are rational abstractions upon the theme of the American sky-

scraper rather than what the American skyscraper itself was—a rational calculation (with trimmings if necessary) as to the worthwhile investment in a given speculation.

We are here at the place where different conceptions as to what is real, rational, and logical exist side by side; and to stigmatize any as being radical or conservative, irrelevant or relevant is not to be very useful. Simply, it is best to say that, while in Chicago certain things (the culmination of an unbridled empiricism?) were done, there was an incapacity and/or refusal to conceive of them in other than specific terms; that they were, therefore, construed without any regard for their proper enormity; that, thus, one has to look to those European skyscrapers which existed only in the imagination to discover any even slightly plausible, public rationale for what Chicago had produced; and that, just as the European innovators of the twenties related the skyscraper not simply to commerce but to a notion of society as a whole—even implying that the skyscraper might be an agent of social salvation—so these same innovators also ascribed an ideal, a general, and an abstract function to the structural frame. In America, the skeleton structure, conceived to be of utilitarian value, had been rationalized by the predominantly utilitarian tone of a Chicago business community; but, in Europe, where simple issues of utility could not assume such prominence, it was given a logical form only by the sustained volition of an architectural intelligentsia. And, for these avowed protagonists of revolution, the frame became something other than what it had been for Chicago. It became an answer not to the specific problem, office building, but to the universal problem, architecture.

Le Corbusier's drawing for the Domino House represents precisely such an evaluation; and is perhaps the perfect illustration of the meaning of the frame for the International Style. What we have here is not so much a structure as an icon, an object of faith which is to act as a guarantee of authenticity, an outward sign of a new order, an assurance against lapse into private license, a discipline by means of which an invertebrate expressionism can be reduced to the appearance of reason.

Disposed to accept the frame as much for reasons of dogma as utility, the International Style was therefore led to envisage it as enforcing a system with which the architect was *obliged* to come to terms; and, for this reason, the exponents of the International Style felt themselves under the necessity of evolving an equation between the demands of space and the demands of the skeleton structure. In Chicago, a comparable obligation could not exist and, therefore, no comparable equation could be reached. There, where the frame served as no more than empirical convenience, it was scarcely to be invested with ideal significance. It could predicate no city of tomorrow. Indeed, by the nineties, it predicated a city of yester-day. Its overtones were not so much prophetic as they were historical; and, since it soon became increasingly possible to see the frame structure as the nakedly irresponsible agent of a too ruthless commercialism, so it became, not around the office building conceived as paradigmatic and normative, but around the alternative program of the residence that idealist and progressivist sentiment was able to effect a coherent expression.

It is by such inferences that Wright's continuous unwillingness to use the frame may possibly be explained. He was too close to it to be able to invest it with the iconographic content which it later came to possess; too close to the Loop to feel other than its abrasiveness and constriction; and too undetached from Chicago to see the city as the idea which it so nearly is and which the reforming mind of the 1920s might have wished it to become.

To attribute an iconographical content to the frame was, for better or worse (and unknowingly) the prerogative of the International Style; and if one can understand how for Mies, preoccupied with anonymity—again with the idea and not the fact—his own self-willed and classical anonymity could be equated with the empirical anonymousness of the Chicago School, one may also perceive how for other exponents and apologists of the International Style, unacquainted with the sociopolitical detail of the Loop, its technical and formal effects must often have been seen as derived from the same details as had comparable effects in Europe. That is, because structural renovation was unconsciously associated with the will to complete social reform, the Loop could be seen as some surreptitious adumbration of a ville radieuse and that therefore an intention could be ascribed to its architects which they did not possess.

But in the Loop, unlike the ville radieuse, the world was accepted as found; and, while it remains ironical that, in terms of forms, this mid-Western acceptance should be so comparable to the discoveries of European protest, it should not be curious that for Wright the forms conceivable as representing protest should have to be sought elsewhere.

## Notes

1 Louis H. Sullivan, *Autobiography of an Idea*, New York, 1924, p. 314.

2 Montgomery Schuyler, "A Critique of the Works of Adler and Sullivan," *Architectural Record*, 1895. Reprinted, William Jordy and Ralph Coe, eds., in *Schuyler, American Architecture and Other Writings*, Cambridge, Mass., 1961, pp. 377-79.

3 Henry Russell Hitchcock, *In the Nature of Materials*, New York, 1942, p. 68.

4 Quoted in Schuyler, p. 381.

5 Schuyler, p. 381.

6 Harriet Monroe, *John Root*, New York, 1968, p. 107.

7 Siegfried Giedion, *Space, Time and Architecture*, Cambridge, Mass., ed. 1941, p. 215.

8 Sullivan, pp. 312-13.

9 Schuyler, p. 382.

10 Le Corbusier, *Towards a New Architecture*, London, 1927, p. 33.

Plate 38   Fair Store, Chicago. William Le
Baron Jenney, 1889-90.

Plate 39   Gale House, Chicago. Frank Lloyd
Wright, 1909.

Plate 40   Schroeder House, Utrecht. Gerrit
Rietveld, 1924.

Plate 41   Second Leiter Building, Chicago.
William Le Baron Jenney, 1889-90.

Plate 42   Project, Luxfer Prism Skyscraper.
Frank Lloyd Wright, 1895.

Plate 43   Project, Press Building. Frank
Lloyd Wright, 1912.

Plate 44   Project, National Life Insurance
Skyscraper. Frank Lloyd Wright, 1924.

Plate 45   Project, St. Mark's Tower. Frank
Lloyd Wright, 1929.

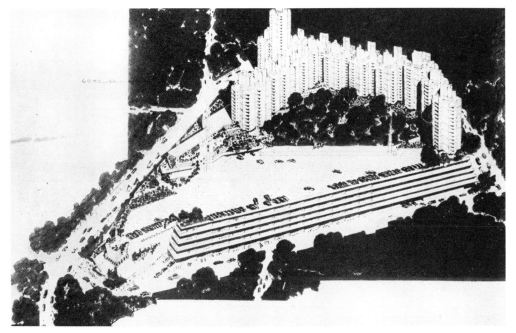

Plate 46   Project, Crystal Heights Hotel.
Frank Lloyd Wright, 1940.

Plate 47   McGlurg Building, Chicago. Holabird and Roche, 1899-1900.

Plate 48   Maison du Peuple, Brussels. Victor
Horta, 1897.

Plate 49   Reliance Building, Chicago. D. H.
Burnham and Company, 1895.

Plate 50   Project, Glass Tower. Ludwig Mies
van der Rohe, 1921.

# Neo-'Classicism' and Modern Architecture I

Written, 1956-57. First published in *Oppositions 1*, 1973.

The Miesian and the Palladian: for some time in certain circles these epithets have been almost synonymous, and now that we are no longer shocked by their juxta-position, and no longer even shocked by our lack of shock, one might well ask what larger issues are subtended by this little semantic revolution. It has been so quiet a coup, so lacking in flags and manifestoes, that one might be tempted to believe it not to have taken place—if only the buildings were not there to prove it, and if innumerable student drawing boards did not seem to promise more to follow.

Nor has there been any unwillingness to recognize these buildings for what they are. Already in 1953, in a house whose symmetry a casual observer might then have dismissed as innocent, *Forum* was ready to detect 'Palladian' overtones; recently the *Architectural Record* has been able to designate similar manifestations as "Space-Time Palladian"; while in England, *The Architectural Review* has from time to time hinted to its readers of the formalistic dangers inherent to a neo-Palladian program. It would thus be ill advised to believe that a new attitude has not appeared, or to assume that the appellation 'Palladian' is not something more than another straw casually blowing in the critical wind.

Most generally the contemporary neo-'Palladian' building presents itself as a small house equipped with Miesian elevations and details. Conceptually a pavilion and usually a single volume, it aspires to a rigorous symmetry of exterior and (where possible) interior. If not Mies's Resor House, then Philip Johnson's Oneto House (Plate 51) at Irvington-on-Hudson may be considered a forerunner of the type, of which John Johansen's house in Fairfield County, Connecticut (Plate 52), and Bolton and Barnstone's De Moustier House in Houston (Plate 53) represent more elaborate examples. But almost certainly other examples, and not necessarily domestic ones, will suggest themselves.

It may be noticed that buildings such as these are a distinctly American phenomenon—or at least that they are scarcely for the moment to be found outside the United States. It may also be suggested that their resemblance to any alleged prototype along the Brenta or around Vicenza is slight, that obviously their architects have eschewed any overt historical reminiscence; but that, being inspired by certain activities of Mies van der Rohe, they have presumed the symmetrical disposition of a building to be adequate for most purposes and that, in doing so, have arrived at some rough approximation of the characteristic Palladian *parti*.

There is not—or perhaps there should not be—anything very remarkable about a Palladian *parti*; some forty or fifty years ago it would conceivably have escaped notice. And there is not—or should not be—anything very much to engage atten-

tion in a small Miesian house which is surely among the more distinguished con-
ventions of the last decade. But this new convention, the small and elegant Miesian house which self-consciously advertises a Palladian *parti,* should still invite
attention; and, in the first case, perhaps not so much for what it is as for what it
signifies.

For twenty years ago a proposal that by the turn of the century the members of
a younger generation of architects might be obsessively fascinated by problems of
symmetry would have appeared dubious—or one presumes it would; while in
1947, one knows, the supposition would still have appeared surprising. In 1937,
with the few, and ten years ago, with the many, it was probably safe to assert
that, among other formalistic aberrations, the 'cult of the axis' was dead, or dy-
ing. But apparently today things have changed; and, as the reflections of this
change, these neo-'Palladian' buildings do seem to propose a question, a problem
that might quite simply be stated thus:

Either we are scarcely able to accept these buildings as examples of modern architecture; or
We are scarcely able to accept modern architecture's theoretical professions.

And, while the first proposition is absurd and the second is distressing, embarrassment still cannot inhibit the suspicion that buildings of this kind do constitute a
decisive breach, not only with modern architecture's *orthodox* tenets, but also
with the visual criteria of what might be considered its canonical achievements.

Because in a general sense this problem concerns some of the more impeccable
and influential productions of the present day it begins to grow acute; and, in any
case, this post-Miesian manner is now altogether too general for it to be lightly
dismissed as a private diversion of the sophisticated. Nor can it be properly judged
in isolation. Almost certainly, for its significance to be understood, it should be
seen as paralleled by that broader, more popular, and dubiously classicizing movement reasonably exemplified by such works as Yamasaki's St. Louis Airport
(Plate 54) and Saarinen's auditorium and chapel group at M.I.T. (Plate 55).

These developments—the domestic interpretation of Mies in terms of a latter
day Pompeian amenity and the quasi-Roman translation lately given to the experiments of Nervi, Buckminster Fuller, and Candela—are evidently related. Thus,
although the one is involved primarily with the plan and the other shows perhaps
a more developed interest in structure, both are preoccupied with an ideal of volumetric control, both display a partiality for centralized space, both show an ur-

bane and technocratic rather than a rustic and craftsmanlike conception of architecture, and neither has any quarrel with the present day. But, while indisputably
both depend on the so-called International Style, it is a little too easy to assert
that they represent no more than an extension of the sanctions of this 'style.' A
reaction *à l'antique* such as this has been recognized to be, such a reaction, carried
out within the framework of modern architecture and sometimes with a belliger-
ent loyalty towards it—on the face of it this is so odd and so much a violation of
what was thought to be the idea of modern architecture that it deserves a serious
attention.

Of course what is, or what was thought to be, the *idea* of modern architecture is
a subject of some confusion—as such matters always must be. Also, and in order
to establish any standard of judgment, to refer to an orthodox theory of modern
architecture is unwarrantable, to invoke modern architecture's canonical achievements is exaggerated, while even to imply the existence of the International Style
is somewhere to give offense. Nevertheless, it is for the moment a convenience to
use all these terms as implements of criticism, as working generalizations in order
to permit a few ideas to be deployed; and although such generalizations will
scarcely respect the thickness of texture which is present in the most elementary
situation, if they are understood to be no more than implements they might still
do some rough justice to the facts.

Thus, if modern architecture proposed to combat all vested orthodoxy in the
interests of rational evolution and if it never conceived its past as likely to deter-
mine its future, it is still beyond argument that a certain consensus of theoretical
precept and some common compositional methods did distinguish the verbal pronouncements and plastic solutions of the twenties, and therefore it is not entirely
misleading to speak of the International Style. Further, since the architectural
crystallization of thirty-five years ago still remains of crucial significance, it is not
completely unreasonable to recognize its representative manifestations—the Bauhaus, Garches, the Barcelona Pavilion for instance—as establishing a canon; and
then to identify the theory which inspired these buildings as orthodox.

But orthodox theory, it must be admitted, is not easy to identify. It is apparently something less than a consistent doctrine and something more than a body
of principles. It is an unformulated collection of aphorisms and polemic from
which certain inferences can be drawn. It is an attitude of mind which we may
recognize by its temperature. For present purposes it is that atmosphere of
thought vaguely associated with Le Corbusier, Gropius, and Mies van der Rohe

which expounds and justifies the appearance of a new architecture in the years following 1919.

Persuasive, sometimes contradictory, often highly condensed, precisely because it is a climate of opinion, orthodox theory does not submit itself too readily to analysis. It is like a building which resists frontal examination which, in consequence, one is obliged to approach from the flank; and, so, since it is impossible to approach it head on, it might be as well as a beginning to get into it as it were by surprise and then very briefly to observe one of its central assumptions—a proposition that the condition of a community's architecture is a symptom of its social and spiritual health. This, as the more scientifically stated proposition that the evolution of architecture may be an index to the history of ideas, is obviously one of the more basic postulates of the history of art; but, as a hypothesis that contemporary society is sick, doomed, lacking in integration, chaotic, while the society of the future will be whole, sane, organically differentiated and ordered, it furnishes an invaluable clue to the mind and spirit of an epoch. The world, it seems to imply, awaits the great regeneration; and modern architecture emerges as a kind of present evidence of this, as the result not so much of a change of vision but as the result of a change of heart.

Obviously these suppositions which are not without distinctly theological overtones expanded the feelings and contributed dignity; while, being able to conceive of himself in these millennial terms, the modern architect was able to become a kind of Siegfried or St. George. He became the hero figure who, strangely absolved from contemporary corruption, is the killer of the eclectic dragons which are its symbol and the protagonist not only of an architectural but of a social revolution. And, since by means of reference to these attitudes, the individual building could be understood not simply as a building but as the indication of a genuine rebirth, so it was partly in this way that the International Style, perhaps alone of all the *avant-garde* movements of the twenties, was provided with a basic responsibility. Endowed with a rationale quite independent of architecture, the modern building became a ritual celebration of the humane potential in a mechanized society.

This was an imposing fantasy; and the intensity of commitment which characterized the innovators of the twenties might, without too much exaggeration, be explained in terms of their accepting it. It was a fantasy which provided the new architecture with an ethical content, equipped it with a distinct symbolism, and became highly instrumental in its popular success. But it is now, of course, exactly this popular success which seems to have become injurious to this whole idealization of the future planned world motif. Awkwardly, many of modern architecture's most significant achievements are already of respectable antiquity. One may approach them in much the same state of mind as was formerly reserved for the Palazzo Farnese or the Louvre. We have become aware that modern architecture has a past, not to speak of a present; and since this present—the future of yesterday for which all the struggle was—is not apparently threatened by any imminent Utopia, the whole millennial justification begins to seem embarrassing. Modern architecture is now recognized by governments and endorsed by great corporations. A generation has grown up which accepts it as a matter of course; and, therefore, the modern architect can less seriously claim to be the protagonist of any new integration of culture. He can no longer very well be militant; and, being less disposed to evangelize a world which, without changing very much, has accepted him, he seems now more willing to resume a specific function.

Gain or loss, there is here in this combination of public appreciation, practical success, and a certain deflation of optimism, one of the contributory causes of the new attitudes and one of the possible explanations of that partly obsessive, partly defiant relationship with the older masters which characterizes the present day. The derivative nature of the new movements is apparent and sometimes self-proclaimed. Often they differ from their source material largely by reason of what they have in common with it; and generally they are apt to play upon the same sensibilities.

Neo-'Palladianism,' for instance, has inherited particularly from Mies a sense of propriety. It has adopted particularly from him an ordinance of the building envelope. It has been led by him to accept as sufficient the statement of elementary volume. Its preferred textures, its taste for big scale and immaculate finish are largely Miesian, while it has enjoyed the same sanction for its symmetrical solutions. And to a not so extreme degree the same statements are also true of the less formulated neo-'classical' manner. This has absorbed a number of further elements; it is structurally more adventurous; it is perhaps more disposed to look with favor upon Le Corbusier; but, at the last analysis, its Miesian point of origin is not easy to dispute.

However, the two movements, and the neo-'Palladian' in particular, seem to be most intimately linked with Mies (and with that orthodox theory of which he is here considered a representative) by their characteristically 'typical' and neutral forms. Here, and in the cold synthetic materials by which they chose to realize these forms, their allegiance to a principle of the twenties could scarcely be more explicitly stated. But it may be the explicit nature of this statement which also calls attention to it as an act of compensation—since, quite as explicitly, in their choice of *partis* and by their unashamed selecting of certain forms *in and for themselves*, the new movements set other principles of the twenties at a distance.

"The attempt to revive architecture from the point of view of form appeared to be doomed,"[1] wrote Mies in 1940 of the situation *c.* 1910; and his "We refuse to recognise problems of form but only of building" is almost a battle cry of the years *c.* 1923. It is the *leitmotif* of the Bauhaus and a constantly recurring element, though with different inflection, in the thought of Le Corbusier. The pursuit of form was presumed to lead to forms of doubtful integrity, to be irrational and private, to be a willful preoccupation with the past, an irresponsible sidetracking of the future; and there was the example of the nineteenth century to prove it. The new architecture was to be authentic. That is, it was to be inevitable and predestined and in the nature of things. It was not to be one possibility among many, but the only possibility; and thus it was necessary that its determinants should seem to lie outside the sphere of choice, that what Mies has termed "subjective license" should be eradicated and that, in its place, 'objectivity' should be installed as the criterion of value.

'Objectivity' meant limits. It implied also an impersonal, a generalized and an abstracted form; and, of course, the conception of such a form, purged of individual sentiment and rising above personal emotion, is, at the bottom, a classical one. It is the idea which subsumes all tragic drama. And most notably this aspect of the demand for neutrality seems to have been understood by Le Corbusier. But the same requirement could be given an alternative twist. 'Typical' form could be seen as necessitated by mass production, by common sense, by the reality of everyday and by the demands of a new society. 'Objectivity,' it might seem, could be guaranteed by an exacting attention to use fabrication and performance, by giving to architecture the impersonal purity of a technique; and such form, it was sometimes felt, would, in contrast to the architecture of the last five hundred years, be rational and an answer to the needs of the spirit.

But the discriminating doubted whether this could be all. An architecture which repudiates mere stylishness and willful innovation but which calls itself 'modern,' or 'new,' or for that matter 'contemporary' possibly means something by these words. Their significance is not entirely chronological. An architecture which calls itself 'organic' is apt to invoke biology. A 'modern' architecture, of necessity, calls up a criterion of contemporaneity; and thus, according to Gropius, the new architecture is "the inevitable logical product of the intellectual, social and technical condition of our age";[2] and, although this may mean a great deal, it can also only mean that in order for a building to be 'new' or 'modern' it must embody a full consciousness of certain imperious and strictly contemporary demands, that it must be predicated not only in terms of function, structure and materials but also in terms of that more intangible content: *the spirit of the age.*

It was a valuable idea. It elevated modern architecture above both mere rational-ism and mere whimsy. It was an idea which, seeing modern architecture as the 'inevitable' product of the time, gave it value in terms of all preceding time. It was the standard which Mies called up in 1923-24 when he gave his eloquent defini-tion of architecture as "the will of the epoch transplanted into space." But at the same time and with equal eloquence he had also demanded of architecture that "it should exclusively be: building."

Now there is a possible dichotomy here which it might be said that Mies has ever since been attempting to solve. For, if architecture is to be simply rational building and simultaneously to be the embodiment of the spirit of the age, then we are forced to one of two conclusions: either that the spirit of the age is simply materialist, concerned entirely with technology; or that it is so refined in its powers of selection as to be willing to content itself with a simply technological expression. And, if either of these possibilities seems to be improbable—and both do seem to be unlikely—then it can only be assumed that although modern archi-tecture may be a physical translation of "the will of the epoch" it can scarcely, for that very reason, be simply rational building and no more.

However, since the spirit of the age, while perhaps a reality which can scarcely be disputed, is also a very elastic conception, a discrepancy of this kind can often be overlooked. For, by implication, the spirit of an age is a universal spirit, irre-sistible, suprarational, impersonal, perceptive, and wise. It is, presumably, the unexpressed cravings at any given time of mankind—or 'the people'; so that, in presenting himself as the interpreter of this collective unconscious, the modern architect added a further role to his Siegfried-St. George repertoire. He became now he who intuits what should be, the mediator between the unconscious psy-chological life of the 'folk' and the technological means at its disposal, the seer, the prophet, the guru. He became now not only the protagonist of social renova-tion but also, it might be said, the midwife of history—or of historically signifi-cant form.

Or at least something like this seems to have been the idea; and, obviously, armed in this way and able to see himself as the neutral agent of an epochal will, the innovating architect of the twenties was well able to "refuse to recognise problems of form." These problems were, in theory, no longer his own. Form became now, not the result of choice, but an imperious necessity of evolution or an unavoidable effect of social change; and, in this way, the architect could depersonalize his taste and then interpret it afresh as a prophetic intuition.

But when an aesthetic preference becomes an insight into human destiny it may, for all the overt suppression of its real nature, still flourish as happily as before; and the fact that it may explains a great deal which is otherwise inexplicable. For, logically followed, the rationalist theme of orthodox theory—that of a dedicated architecture determined by use and technology—should have resulted in a series of solutions elicited entirely by inductive and empirical methods, solutions which might happen to be similar by reason of similar functions or similar technological conditions; and the canonical monuments, which have been here too long neglected, are anything but this. They were intended to embody the spirit of the age and of course they did; but, at its most architecturally enlightened, this spirit of the age was also highly defined and, whether it was supposed to or not, it does seem to have prompted forms quite as specific as those neo-'classical' distributions which today are deliberately chosen.

Thus when Gropius writes in 1923 of "a new aesthetic of the horizontal," and when he adds that

at the same time the symmetrical relationship of parts of a building and their orientation towards a central axis is being replaced by a new conception of equilibrium which transmutes this dead symmetry of similar parts into an asymmetrical but equal balance,"[3]

while implying that this is a general tendency (which it certainly was), he also provides some indication of his own quite personal feeling for specific distributions of form.

And, in a remarkably similar passage, so influential a publicist as Theo Van Doesburg displays a comparable preference.

In the course of time the symmetrical composition has pressed itself more and more towards the centre, towards the axis of the plane, to such a degree that the composition is entirely pivot shaped and the canvas remains blank and therefore gives an impression of emptiness.

Very important essential renewal of the method of composition. Gradual abolition of the centre and of all passive emptiness. The composition develops in the opposite direction, instead of towards the centre towards the extreme periphery of the canvas, it even appears as it were to continue beyond it. . . .[4]

Here, though Gropius is writing about architecture and Van Doesburg ostensibly about painting, both are saying very much the same thing. Van Doesburg stigma-

tizes symmetry and proposes "the abolition of the centre"; Gropius finds traditional symmetry "dead" and being replaced by " a new conception of equilibrium"; Van Doesburg concludes this 'new equilibrium' to be concerned with peripheric rather than concentric developments; and the evidences of what he elsewhere called "peripheric composition" are to be recognized in varying degrees in
most of the historically significant buildings of the period—whatever their functions, whatever their structure, whatever their materials.

Peripheric composition, because of a mental set against the exercise of aesthetic
preference, was rarely acknowledged; but, whether consciously employed or not,
it does seem to have provided a major principle of organization. When Siegfried
Giedion writes of the Bauhaus that it "expands into a pin wheel" or that "the
ground floor lacks all tendency to contract inwards upon itself,"[5] he identifies
one of its manifestations. When Philip Johnson notices that in Mies's earlier buildings "the unit of design is no longer the cubic room but the free standing wall,
sliding out from beneath the roof and extending into the landscape," he recognizes another. But at Garches the "abolition of the centre" is conducted in even
more thoroughgoing fashion than at either the Bauhaus or the Barcelona Pavilion,
and there, particularly, the full relevance of the peripheric idea becomes evident.

At Garches (Plate 7), precisely because of the condensation of the building into
a block, that centralization to which Gropius and Van Doesburg were so averse
seems certainly to be demanded. But the strongly repetitive nature of the grid—
the basic constituent of so many modern buildings—tends to prohibit it. And the
sandwichlike layers of space—also a product of the grid—have the same effect.
They emphasize the idea of an extension, of a pulling outwards rather than a concentration of space; and, while it is true that at Garches a gesture is made towards
centralization by the perforation of the floor slabs and the inflection of the grid
to an ABABA rhythm, Le Corbusier's solution remains the classic illustration of
how peripheric composition was able to reinforce seemingly intrinsic characteristics of the skeleton structure. It enters into a contrapuntal relationship with this
skeleton; and, by doing so, it further deemphasizes the already unemphatic center
of the building and strengthens or gives tension to the extremities of the space.

Nor, obviously, was peripheric composition merely the practice of modern
architects of the great generation. Just as clearly it may be seen persisting in one
of the most representative American buildings of c. 1947—in Marcel Breuer's
Robinson House at Williamstown, Massachusetts (Figure 10), a binuclear scheme
of considerable finesse, providing an almost perfect example of how the predis-
positions of the twenties became progressively modified by an increased taste for

Figure 10   Robinson House, Williamstown,
Mass. Plan. Marcel Breuer, 1947.

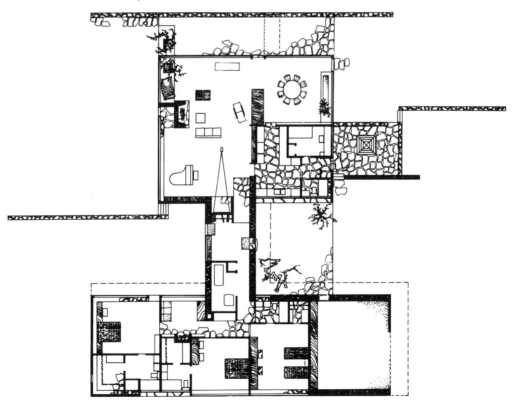

the rustic. Theoretically a diagram derived from analysis of function underlies the conception of any such house as this one; but, after any more than a casual inspection of Breuer's building, it becomes evident that the existence of its two cores is not only a matter of their use but is also a method of building up a spatial tension. And it further becomes clear that the comparative insignificance of the central link connecting the two cores is not only an expression of its minor purpose but primarily is the means to instigate that series of visual excitements which are to be discovered around the edges of the composition. While, finally, it is seen to be these peripheric incidents—low walls, extruded roofs, slits and slots—which contribute a particular stringency to the building, define its air of modernity, and predetermine our sensations of pleasure.

Precisely because the peripheric principle (which, according to prejudices, might be traced back to Cubist painting, and/or *De Stijl*, and/or the Prairie houses of Frank Lloyd Wright) was so compatible with technical media and functional planning, because it could generate products so various and legitimate as a Garches, a Bauhaus, and a Barcelona Pavilion, there was in the 1920s and later no immediate need to recognize its independent and active role. Indeed, to have done so would have seriously damaged modern architecture's polemic. And while orthodox theory could at any time (presumably by appealing to the spirit of the age) have legitimated peripheric composition, it preferred not to do this—and understandably so. Up to a point, orthodox theory has been highly effective. It has been propagandist and evangelical; and, in calling up the spirit of the age, it provided itself with a most formidable ally. But this ally, which was an essential catalyst of the International Style, was also expected to remain a somewhat remote presiding deity. It was to inaugurate a 'new vision'; but, otherwise, its behavior was not seriously to affect a rationalistic program. Thus, there arose the anomaly of a theory which seemed to be unable but which was really only unwilling to provide adequate explanation of the phenomena which it purported to sponsor; and there appeared that dilemma to which Matthew Nowicki called attention, the problem "that even when form results from a functional analysis this analysis follows a pattern that leads to the discovery of the same function whether in a factory or a museum."[6]

A glossing over of this problem, as Nowicki well recognized, is of no service to modern architecture; platitudes will not conceal it; and when it is perceived, as it is generally perceived, to what degree functional and structural analysis has been consistently edited so as to facilitate the expression of a preference, then, however acceptable the results might be, apprehension necessarily follows as to how precarious are the philosophical foundations of such activity. Now a precarious philosophical foundation may be neither here nor there, may sometimes in no way impede the most remarkable performance, may occasionally be positively advantageous; but, in spite of this, the lack of correlation between compositional practice and the explanation of it which was becoming glaringly apparent by the late 1940s almost certainly did provide a prompting for the developments under discussion.

To make a metaphor: it might be said that rationalist theory, understood to be a scheme of determinism *qua* function and technology, had entered into a gentleman's agreement *c.* 1922-23 with a grand historical abstraction; and that rationalist theory, perhaps, had not fully understood the consequences. Nor was it any mere arrangement of convenience which brought the two together; since, in order that a rationalist architecture might become a 'new' one, it was essential that the spirit of the age should be embraced. And, apparently, the agreement was successful. The one partner was analytical. The other dynamic. And both were stimulated. But there was a potential incompatibility in the amalgam; dimly, this seems to have been suspected. The spirit of the age can be indiscreet. Rationalism never. But the two shared many of the same interests. The spirit of the age was an enthusiast for speed, mass production, airplanes, reinforced concrete, sociology, sunbathing, heavy machinery, simple life, factories, grain elevators, Atlantic liners, hygiene, and the classic automobiles which were created in its own image; and, so long as it could be believed that the creature was aesthetically neutral, rationalism was not eager to discourage such discriminating excess. But, when the first evidences of *taste* were revealed, the old problem which the partnership had been established to settle was back again; and, for rationalism in general, the recognition that the epoch's will is not something entirely transcendental, philanthropic, or practical has been the source of acute embarrassment. The lapse into consciousness has meant the end of innocence.

This metaphor has been intended to point out the dilemma which can result from advocating a dual doctrine and failing to recognize its duality. The attempt to relate the spirit of the age to the function-structure-materials triad was entirely understandable. But, in reality, these are natural antitheses and not harmonious partners. They are the positive and negative charges which authenticate any genuine process of creation. But they can be brought together only in a relationship of tension. Neither can be subordinated to the other. They are both autonomous and require constant check. And, by the late 1940s, so much could be intuited. For by then it had become evident, in more ways than one, that the spirit of the age was not entirely to be trusted. Certainly it was no longer the tractable and stimulating playmate which, twenty years earlier, it had seemed to be. In architecture it had proved itself more than competent to outmaneuver an unsuspecting rationalism. Nor was it exactly impartial; and, if the spirit of the age could show a taste for peripheric composition, it might equally well develop one for Corinthian capitals and/or pointed arches; and if then, as Nowicki had suggested, function, structure, and materials were no more than the pragmatic sanctions of architectural form, how could they resist it? They scarcely could; and, as a result, rationalism was distinctly embarrassed.

The attempts to resolve this dilemma have been many. The postwar Italian idea was simply to be witty about it. In England, picturesque townscape provided a characteristically national escape route down which hundreds fled. In the United States, regionalism, by attempting to set up the spirit of the province as a check to the spirit of the age, provided one characteristically American solution. But this form of architectural states' rights could scarcely exist without the complement of a central authority; and, as a version of this central authority, the present neo-'Classical' mutations must appear to any dispassionate observer to be no less typically American.

Briefly, being somewhat disturbed about the spirit of the age, the new movements apparently propose to submit their fictional or real demands to arbitration. To the question which Nowicki asked of the canonical works—Are these buildings the rationalization of function-structure-materials and no more? Or are they the product of a specific aesthetic originating at a certain time?—they have replied with unaffected casualness. They have reserved judgment on function, if not on structure and materials; and, while they are, conceivably, aware of an aesthetic which originated in particular places at a certain time, they are indisposed to attribute to it inordinate significance. Rather the reverse. Disposed to keep this aesthetic at some distance, they do so at the level of taste by reemphasizing a form of concentric composition, and at the level of ideas by attempting to assert a universal principle—one to which both the less instructed and the members of a real or supposed elite may alike give assent. Thus, they have assumed the existence of an idea applicable at all times; and, in doing so, they imply an intention to subordinate the imperatives of the epoch to an architectural equivalent of the rule of law.

Exception can scarcely be taken to the logic or to the responsibility of this conservative but eminently radical step. It is one of the limited ways of plugging a gap which has become more and more insupportable. It is the product of personalities which require a standard; but which, unwilling to be left to the mercies of the time-spirit, are equally unwilling to be left to those of nature. That is: it is the product of personalities which cannot accept an 'organic' incursion into Wrightian territory as a possible solution; and, instead, neo-'Classicism' has taken its stand in favor of the legislative ability of mildly Platonic forms, with the presumption that these are valid independent of function or technique and that, while they may defer to the age, in theory at least, they transcend it.

Very little more need now be said. On the face of it the neo-'Classical' choice might have brought those who chose into the orbit of Le Corbusier who, perhaps anticipating a problem of this kind, very long ago proclaimed his decided adherence to immutable laws of geometry and mathematics. But that a different allegiance was declared is accountable. Miesian example is more accessible, more suited to advanced technology; and, in addition, Mies had gradually modified his position with regard to his 'will of the epoch' which, apparently unrestricted in 1923, had by 1930 become substantially qualified. By 1930 he could announce:

**The new era is a fact: it exists, irrespective of our "yes" or "no." It is neither better nor worse than any other era. It is pure datum, in itself without value content. . . . One thing will be decisive, the way we assert ourselves in the face of circumstance.**

And, if by 1930 the value of an individual assertion was set up against what in 1923 seems to have been a collective one, by 1938 Mies had defined his position further. In his inaugural address at the Illinois Institute of Technology he is able to propose a distinction between "practical aims" and "values"; and it becomes now only by the first that "we are bound to the specific structure of our time" while the second are now assumed to be "rooted in the spiritual nature of man."

This gradual revision of what, in the first case, appeared to be a crudely deterministic position has given Mies a peculiar centrality at the present time. He has gradually pulled away from the less tenable defenses of modern architecture; but, if he seems now to conceive of architecture as arising from the interaction of a specific contemporary technology and an unchanging spiritual nature, one might guess that the neo-'Classical' movements are only half disposed to agree. They have received certain idealized forms as a gift from Chicago, and they have received them with the difficult proviso that "form is not the aim of our work but only the result." They are apt to respect this proviso but also to beg to differ. Possibly less disillusioned than Mies with "the will of the epoch," they are less disposed than he to restrict it to matters of technology. But, still anxious to control it, they wish to employ Miesian form precisely for this purpose—as a reasonable restraint which might hint at a conviction expressed through an attitude.

It is not, it might be suggested, so much a spiritual or an architectural conviction, as a social, almost a sociological one. "Nothing is more pitiful than the arrogant disdain of our contemporaries for questions of form," wrote de Tocqueville in the 1830s, and the cogency of his observation to the point at issue must excuse the introduction of this august personage. "Men living in democratic ages do not readily comprehend the utility of forms" he adds; and, though his primary reference is to social and political forms, form in itself is also implied. "Democratic nations naturally stand more in need of form than any other nations," he continues. "In aristocracies," he concludes, "the observance of forms was superstitious: among us they ought to be kept up with a deliberate and enlightened deference."[7]

If it is not too facetious to suppose that this kind of argument is implied by a number of post-Miesian buildings, it would be of some interest to know to what it might lead.

## Notes

1 All quotations from Mies van der Rohe are to be found in Philip Johnson, *Mies van der Rohe*, New York, 1947.

2 Walter Gropius, *Scope of Total Architecture*, New York, 1955, p. 61. Reprinted from the *R. I. B. A. Journal*, London, 1934.

3 Herbert Bayer, Walter Gropius, Ilse Gropius, *Bauhaus 1919-28*, New York, 1938.

4 From *De Stijl VII* pp. 24-7. See also *De Stijl*, Cat. 81, Stedelijk Museum, Amsterdam 1951, p. 34.

5 Siegfried Giedion, *Space, Time and Architecture*, Cambridge, Mass., ed. 1941, pp. 495, 497.

6 Matthew Nowicki, "Origins and Trends in Modern Architecture," *Magazine of Art*, November, 1951, p. 273.

7 Alexis de Tocqueville, *Democracy in America*, New York, 1954, Vol. II, p. 344.

Plate 51   Oneto House, Irvington-on-Hudson,
N.Y. Philip Johnson, 1951.

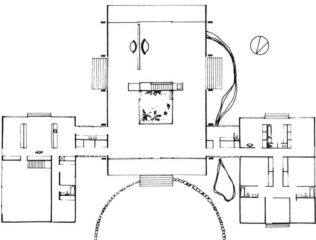

Plate 52   Goodyear House, Fairfield County,
Conn. John Johansen, 1956.

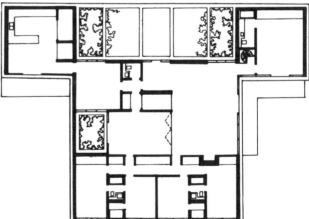

Plate 53  De Moustier House, Houston,
Texas. Bolton and Barnstone.

Plate 54   Airport, St. Louis. Hellmuth,
Yamasaki and Leinweber, 1955.

Plate 55   Kresge Auditorium and Chapel,
Cambridge, Mass. Eero Saarinen, 1953.

# Neo-'Classicism' and
# Modern Architecture II

Written, 1956-57. First published in *Oppositions 1*, 1973.

**The idealistic principle of order . . . with its over emphasis on the ideal and formal, satisfies neither our interest in simple reality nor our practical commonsense.**
**—Mies van der Rohe[1]**

The expressed tastes of a younger generation provide an ironic commentary upon the Miesian text. For, if "the idealistic principle of order" has not lately been set up, then something very close to it evidently has; and paradoxically, it is Miesian example which has provided the incentive for the change. Thus 'ideal' volumetric simplicity, 'ideal' symmetry, and 'ideal' centralization have now become the order of the day; the Greek Revival inspires increased affection; and the disturbed ghost of Palladio threatens to become a frequent visitor in the more discriminating suburbs.

It is particularly such a structure as Crown Hall (Plate 56), the architecture building at the Illinois Institute of Technology, which has seemed to the historically sensitive to be some mid-twentieth century counterpart of the Villa Rotonda; and, since it is symmetrical, four square, and approached by an elevated platform which might suggest the podium of some yet unbuilt portico, it is surely not by accident that it invites the parallel to be drawn. And since, different though they may be, because in the case of each building one senses the activity of an architect who is remorselessly determined to be clear, who is willing to operate only within the most stringent of self-imposed limitations, and who is absolutely concerned with a specific theme, the parallel may be sustained.

But, when all this has been said, and for all its classical implication, Crown Hall is not the Villa Rotonda—nor anything like it. It may occasionally be useful to see this building and its immediate predecessors in this way—that is, if some partial explanation for the recent revival of the Palladian *parti* is demanded; but, for the moment, it would be more profitable to recognize that the Villa Rotonda and (perhaps) Crown Hall are really exemplars of that 'demonstration' of which Louis Sullivan's mathematics teacher spoke, the "demonstration so broad that it will admit of no exceptions";[2] and, since demonstrations of this sort are apt to command the imagination, there is here then some very obvious reason for the phenomenal success which Mies's current conception of architecture has come to enjoy. Apparently so much more crystallized and systematic than the compositional methods of ten, twenty, thirty years ago, it seems now to be reducing these to insignificance. It has the power to impose itself; and, while whether it can succeed in doing so is a matter of importance, whether its success can or will lead to a highly widespread new 'classicism' is scarcely less so.

Shortly after coming to the United States, or perhaps before, Mies obviously reacted very sharply against the elaborately interwoven space compositions which had formerly typified fully developed examples of modern architecture. His spaces became less tense. His rationalism became more acute. In certain ways he may be said to have turned back to that Schinkelesque, Biedermayer neo-Grec which characterized the earlier phases of his career; and, because this evolution seems to have been a crucial one for all the later developments which have absorbed his influence, it might be as well to examine it in some detail.

Since it has been widely asserted that modern architecture is not merely an attitude of mind towards technological and sociological problems but that there has taken place a radical reorientation in the capacity to conceive of space, and since it is implied that, while the elements of this new spatial order may all have been present for many years, their effective synthesis was an achievement of the twenties, it will be useful to clarify certain precepts of what will here be called (for the want of any better term) International Style space. International Style space will here be understood as the space of Garches, of Mies's house for the 1931 Berlin Building Exhibition (Figure 11) and of Le Corbusier's foyer for the Centresoyus Building, Moscow (Figure 12)—to name only a few outstanding examples. All of these are manifestations of the spatial revolution of the twenties. All of them have exercised and continue to exercise a wide influence upon practice; and, although the spatial strategy which they represent has only rarely been achieved, the idea of this space is none the less significant for that.

Like all other systems of space that of the International Style resulted from a reappraisal of the functions attributed to the column, the wall, and the roof; and, at its most developed, it postulated a skeleton structure whose function of support was to be separately expressed from any nonstructural function of enclosure. The skeleton structure, it was recognized, had made bearing walls or the appearance of such walls redundant; and, since this structure was now to be made clear, it was demanded that columns be disengaged from walls and be left free to rise through the open space of the building. All else was a logical deduction. Detached from the liberated columns, the walls were now to become a series of freely disposed screens; and, while in this way there ensued the 'free' plan, its corollary, the 'free' facade, was required—so as to make, by an extensive opening up of the building, a further assertion of the functional independence of its parts.

The principles of this space were perhaps first fully enunciated by Le Corbusier who, around 1926, published a series of diagrams which at that time represented to him the logical effects of a ferroconcrete system;[3] but, about the same date, almost identical conclusions seem to have been reached by Mies with reference to

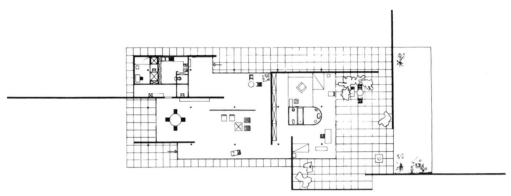

Figure 11   Building Exposition House, Berlin. Plan. Ludwig Mies van der Rohe, 1931.

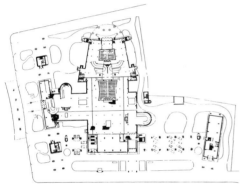

Figure 12   Palais du Centresoyus, Moscow. Plan. Le Corbusier, 1928-32.

the problems presented by steel supports. With Le Corbusier the new demands were put into words, and the new roles ascribed to column, wall, plan, and facade were followed by a new demand with regard to the roof. For both pragmatic and sentimental reasons this was to be flat—so that it could be used as a garden; but obviously—garden or not—flatness of silhouette was also preferred by Mies, not to mention Gropius and innumerable others, and conceivably it was preferred because it was felt to be highly expressive of the peculiarities of the volume which the roof now protected.

For there are other peculiarities of International Style space, some intrinsic, some extrinsic, which deserve attention. As already noticed in the previous essay, it was characterized by a tendency to emphasize a peripheric rather than a central expression of the building. To refer again to Van Doesburg, the center was to be gradually abolished and the composition was to be developed in the opposite direction. Or to paraphrase Gropius, the new demand led to the dead symmetry of similar parts being transmuted into an asymmetrical but equal balance.

Further it should be noticed that, on the whole, International Style space was a system which tended to prohibit any display of beams; and, rather than the *upper* surface of the roof slab being flat, it seems even more certainly to have been required that the *under* surfaces of the roofs and floors should present uninterrupted planes. And this restriction seems to have been a further deduction from the conception of the freedom of the column—since the free column could scarcely assume an explicit relationship with the beams which it might happen to support without leading to a compartmentalizing of space and thus to a violation of something of the freedom of the plan. In fact, the appearance of beams could only tend to prescribe fixed positions for the partitions; and, since these fixed positions would be in line with the columns, it was therefore essential, if the independence of columns and partitions was to be asserted with any eloquence, that the underside of the slab should be expressed as an uninterrupted horizontal surface.

Fundamentally, therefore, in Mies's and Le Corbusier's buildings of c. 1929 the column acts as the punctuation of a horizontally extended space which, particularly with Mies, is characterized by a neutral equality of section. In these buildings the column does not promote the spatial expression of the structural bay, nor do a series of columns define individual structural cells. Rather the reverse is true. The column is no more than an interpolation, a *caesura* in a general space, and the spatial expression of the structural bay is strictly subordinated to a spatial expression of the flat slab which the columns support.

It was probably Mies who provided the most literally perfect transcription of this delicate and complex system of logic; and, by comparison, Le Corbusier may seem to have been less loyal to the principles which he had affirmed. For where Mies's distinctions between functions of support and enclosure are conceptually immaculate, Le Corbusier's may seem often quite perfunctory. But, on the other hand, while the charm of Mies's spaces at this date lay in their peculiarly limpid quality, in their lyrical sensitiveness to the most expensive materials, Le Corbusier seems to have explored a dimension of the problem with which Mies was not concerned. Where Mies's vertical planes trail out suggestively, 'peripherically,' into the landscape, Le Corbusier had already denied himself this possibility. Perhaps out of antipathy to the idea or perhaps out of some instinctive recognition that the principles of a Prairie house could not be so readily fused with the repetitive ordinance of a steel or concrete structure, he had always been predisposed to internalize this peripheric incident—as, for instance, at Garches, where all the long walls which contribute a rotary, pinwheeling movement to Mies's buildings are condensed into the compass of a single block within which they acquire an explosive, emphatic, enriched quality, completely distinguished from the relaxed Miesian serenity.

It is part of the irony of recent developments that, in the 1920s, when Mies had absolutely no use for the block, Le Corbusier could employ it in order to achieve a formulation of International Style space; but that, in the 1940s, Mies should approach a comparable block with a completely different end in view. Apparently Mies had to wait until he arrived in Chicago before the block became with him an obsession; and it is then that his feeling for it became part of his reaction against the spatial order to which he had earlier subscribed. Throughout the early thirties Mies had been progressively simplifying his somewhat overextended manner of 1929-31, and in his patio houses of this time (Figure 13) he had already been led to a retraction of the planes which formerly slipped out from beneath the slab. But, despite this simplification, he still retained a hankering for a somewhat picturesque loose volume, and it is not until Chicago that the block appears—when it is by no means that *prisme pur* to which, fifteen or twenty years earlier, Le Corbusier had expressed his devotion. Instead, Mies's block was very much a version of the old and structurally articulated buildings of the Chicago school; and, most significantly, in acquiring this taste he seems to have acquired also an antipathy for his earlier conception of the column.

Le Corbusier's characteristic column was and has remained circular. Mies's characteristic German column was circular or cruciform; but his new column became H-shaped, became that I-beam which is now almost a personal signature. Typically, his German column had been clearly distinguished from walls and windows, isolated from them in space; and, typically, his new column became an element integral with the envelope of the building, where it came to function as a kind of mullion or residue of wall. Thus the column section was not without some drastic effects on the entire space of the building.

The circular or cruciform section had tended to push partitions away from the column. The new section tended to drag them towards it. The old column had offered a minimum of obstruction to a horizontal movement of space; but the new column presents a distinctly more substantial stop. The old column had tended to cause space to gyrate around it, had been central to a rather tentatively defined volume; but the new column instead acts as the enclosure or the external definition of a major volume of space. The spatial functions of the two are thus completely differentiated. The new column is no longer the old International Style mark of punctuation. Instead it implies the existence of an autonomous structural cell; and any series of such columns now come to function as a kind of skeletalized partition or discontinuous wall.

From this simultaneous affirmation of the block and transformation of the column—whether it was audacious or innocent—all else may be said to flow. As an International Style element the column put in its last appearance in the museum project of 1942 (Figure 14); while in the Library and administration building project of 1944 (Figure 15) the effects of the H-shaped column are already apparent and are clearly exhibited in the published drawings of its plans. From these drawings it is evident that the column is no longer to be allowed to float ambiguously beneath a slab. It is now—apparently for the first time—tied to a network of beams, and these beams have appointed definite positions for the screens, and for the most part the screens have already leapt into these positions. In fact, only the extra-thick walls around the lavatories seem to have been able to resist the new attraction.

So innovative is this achievement that it is a temptation to believe that even Mies himself must have been alarmed by what he had here done. He had produced major symmetrical projects before, but he had produced them largely in terms of his older concept of the column; while in both the Reichsbank and Krefeld projects he had been careful to articulate his principal volumes as separate entities. And now, eschewing this possibility, he had thrown his spaces together so as to comprise as far as possible a continuous whole; but, at the same time, he had refused to allow himself the typical International Style treatment of such continuous space.

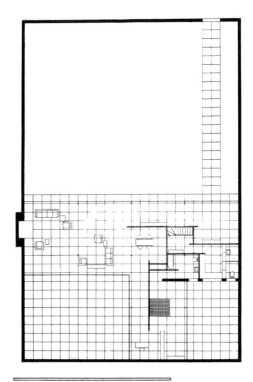

Figure 13   Project, patio house. Plan. Mies
van der Rohe, 1931.

Figure 14   Project, Museum for a Small City.
Plan. Mies van der Rohe, 1942.

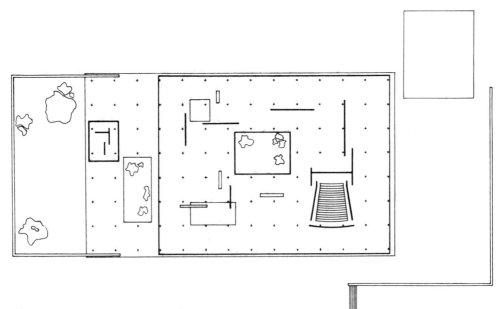

Figure 15   Project, Library and Administration Building, Illinois Institute of Technology, Chicago. Plan. Mies van der Rohe,
1944.

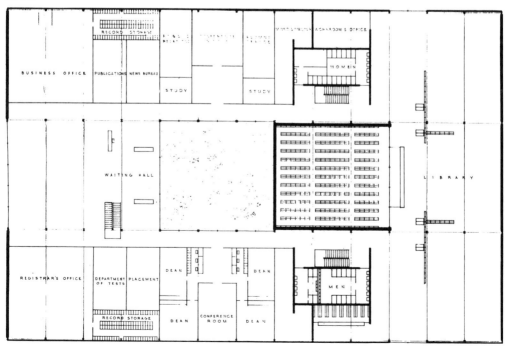

The concept of his new column was both more structural and more classical than that of the revolutionary and plastic column of the twenties; and, having stipulated the column in these terms, Mies could scarcely escape the consequences of his statement. Structural and spatial expression now promised to become more integral than before; but the space, for all its openness, promised to become more rigid. Thus the Library and Administration Building is already puckered by little points of central emphasis, quasi articulations in terms of structure, and it is already tentatively furrowed by a system of axes and cross axes. At any moment it seems about to break down into a scheme of three parallel halls, and again to submit itself to a further breakdown into a constellation of individuated structural cells. The building is like a solution which, upon the addition of a further ingredient, will completely change its nature. But this is not allowed to happen. To prevent it, to hold the solution in suspension, Mies returns again to the concept of the flat slab and floats a false ceiling beneath the greater part of his beams, only allowing them to show at their junctions with the columns. And thus, by restating the space as a rather fattened version of the sandwich volume of which he had been such a master, he was still able to control the quite anomalous developments within it.

But it had been a near thing. The Library and Administration Building is somewhat like a signpost pointing in two or possibly three directions; and, by 1946, in the Farnsworth House and the Drive-in Restaurant projects (Plate 57) the most congenial of these seems to have been chosen. By a considerable expansion of the structural bay, by an expression of the building as a single structural cell, the ossification of space which the new column seemed to threaten could be avoided; and, by an externalizing of the beam, the 'ideal' flatness of the undersurface of the slab could be preserved. But it could be preserved only at the price of emptying the interior as much as possible of all local spaces. For, with the structural bay thus augmented, the organizing ability of the steel skeleton was necessarily diminished. There was less of it. It could no longer therefore provide a repetitive beat, a tempo, for the building. Nor could it any longer very ably control an asymmetrical organization of screens; and, in the columnless space of the later forties, these screens which—as mementoes of the structurally irrelevant walls—had survived as elements of considerable episodic charm now begin to seem embarrassing. Fairly massive cores might be located in this empty space and screens might be disposed with reference to these—but, by the time of the Drive-in Restaurant and Farnsworth House, to all intents and purposes (since it is a combination of their themes) we have returned to the Architecture Building of ten years later; and, in returning to it, we have returned to the resurrected Palladio and to all the problems of neo-'Classicism' which prompted this digression.

Like the characteristic Palladian composition, Crown Hall is a symmetrical and, probably, a mathematically regulated volume. But, unlike the characteristic Palladian composition, it is not an hierarchically ordered organization which projects its centralized theme vertically in the form of a pyramidal roof or dome. Unlike the Villa Rotonda, but like so many of the compositions of the twenties, Crown Hall is provided with no effective central area within which the observer can stand and comprehend the whole. The observer may understand a good deal of the interior while he is external to it (although even this Mies is disposed to disallow by planting a screen of trees across the front); but, once inside, rather than any spatial climax, the building offers a central solid, not energetically stated it is true, but still an insulated core around which the space travels laterally with the enclosing windows. Also, the flat slab of the roof induces a certain outward pull; and, for this reason, in spite of the centralizing activity of the entrance vestibule, the space still remains, though in very much simplified form, the rotary, peripheric organization of the twenties, rather than the predominantly centralized composition of the true Palladian or classical plan.

Nevertheless, in apparently leading up to this plan and then backing away from it, Mies does seem to have created an appetite for it; and thus, on the one hand, in Connecticut there has reemerged the old scheme of *corps de logis* and flanking pavilions and, on the other hand, in Cambridge there has reappeared an image of that relentlessly ideal dome which, whether it is sponsored by Brunelleschi or Buckminster Fuller, appears always to be the unavoidable offspring of an insufficiently prepared flirtation with the classical tradition.

Certainly, at a theoretical level, such a house as Johansen's in Fairfield County and such a structure as Saarinen's Kresge Auditorium at M.I.T. may be said to propose the same formal problem—that of how to assert centrality in the face of circumstances; and in each building a discontinuity between function and expression testifies to the difficulties of an attempt to accommodate this post-Miesian appetite. In Fairfield County the Farnsworth House is triplicated and becomes bedrooms-living room-garage; at M.I.T. a single structural cell like that of the Architecture Building is made triangular, is domed, and is then converted into a receptacle for a concert hall. In Fairfield County, by the inference of the *parti*, either a subordination of the wings to the center or of all three elements to the courtyard is presumed but scarcely could have been expressed without a less diagrammatic handling of structure; and at M.I.T. it is almost the same problem in reverse. Structure there asserts centralization but the plan can hardly accept it.

And, since the anomaly of both these cases obliges one to believe that each of these buildings is really an adjunct to a more general theorem, it is hard not to conclude that the reappearance of vaults and domes is other than a corollary manifestation to the reappearance of highly academic *partis*. The dome, of course, having recently acquired technological legitimacy, is now provided with an empirical justification, while the value of a Palladian plan can scarcely be other than ideal; but when, for all this, one observes how Saarinen has slipped an 'ideal' plan beneath his 'empirical' dome and how Johansen has 'empiricized' his 'ideal' distribution by balancing garage against bedrooms, then one recognizes that there are here two disguises of the same manifestation, that Saarinen's dome is really the consummation of Johansen's spatial demand.

But if the dome, as a form where structural system and spatial expression are completely integral, is the logical conclusion of all attempts to centralize space, it is not necessarily either the inevitable or the desirable one; nor is it altogether a tractable subject. Demanding a completely unified space and the entire suspension of everyday function beneath it, the dome—except as a kind of episodic blister—is altogether too pure a form to accommodate anything except the extreme case; while the post-Miesian architect, above all, has inherited a concern for the typical condition rather for any extreme. Moreover, a dome requires to be seen in complete isolation, to be the whole building—an exceptionally difficult proposition— or it requires the rest of the building to be hierarchically subordinate to it—a proposition which, at the present day, is probably no less difficult.

It is for reasons such as these, which illuminate the results of an unsuspecting pursuit of symmetry and centralization, that one returns to Crown Hall with increased respect and begins to understand all over again how, by still insisting on the flatness of the underside of the slab and by refusing to tolerate the presence of more than one block, Mies has been able to equilibrate both an outward pull and a centralizing moment. And the equilibrium between peripheric and central emphasis, though largely unnoticed, is significant because it does prompt the question of how, with the ingredients of modern building such as they are, can any real or total centralization be made effective. Symmetry maybe, as Mies, Le Corbusier and others have shown. But centralization? To make this effective is surely a logical impossibility. The repetitive nature of the grid which, in spite of casual deviations and very specific programs, remains and is likely to remain the basic component of modern architecture, resists the idea. The horizontal and vertical system of coordinates which the grid provides will scarcely allow any but the most minor differentiation in the form of its members. It insists that rank of all parts of the building should be approximately equal; and, the staccato ordinance of the gridded structure being thus abundantly democratic, how can those almost imperceptible gradations which establish one part of a building as superior to the rest be introduced? Evidently they scarcely can, or scarcely can without subterfuge; and thus it is less with some historically remote Palladian villa but rather with Garches that Crown Hall deserves to be compared.

At Garches, as already observed and emphasized, there is—in an elaborate and now almost antique version—some pragmatic justification for the peripheric composition of the twenties. For, if the centralized theme is virtually put out of bounds by structural means, then, if the building is not to be aesthetically entirely passive, only the absolute opposite of the centralized theme survives as a possibility. Hence International Style space. And even when the free-standing column, one of the essential components of this space at its most developed, is abolished, and when, as in Crown Hall, the monumental structural cell absorbs the whole building, still centralization remains no less difficult. For, like the dome of which it is a flattened, squared out version, a structural cell such as this one is apt to require the sacrifice of all spatial detail and the presence within it of simply an unsegregated void.

In other words, whatever its merits, as a model, Crown Hall is probably too pure to be useful. It may be a statement magnificent in its single-mindedness; but, while it persuades the spirit, it scarcely accommodates the flesh. For unhappily, the empirical world is not reducible to such simplicity; and though we might wish it could be, though we might wish certain aspects of reality (as here) to be, apparently, transcended, Crown Hall does not altogether allay doubts as to whether, in its presence, we are not being lured down some important street which, in spite of appearances, we shall finally discover to be a *cul-de-sac*.

But, if Crown Hall may elicit such questions as these, if its interplay of centrifugal and centripetal stress may not be very visible, if the peripheric idea which Gropius implied and Van Doesburg asserted more than thirty years ago may be shown to be practically reasonable, if centralization and attempts at centralization may be deduced to be impossible, if these are the logical arguments, does this really help? One is reminded of a passage in which Henry Adams quotes Poincare: "How shall I answer the question whether Euclidian geometry is true or false? It has no sense! . . . Euclidian geometry is and will remain the most convenient";[4] and, with regard to centralization, almost the same thing might be said. Neither true nor false, functionally preposterous, being psychologically convenient, it has become a demand; and, as a demand, it provides some explanation for those anti-

Miesian and sometimes astructural gestures in which disciples of Mies have lately been indulging. For, if the repetitive grid obviously predicates a space without focus and if the single enlarged structural cell, while it will permit focus, predicates a space without function, then, if there exists a genuine desire to introduce focus, it might be expected that, after a certain point, *something must give*—either spatial preference, or structure, or both.

There is thus some very good reason for those decorative vaults which have lately compromised the cellular emptiness. Their appearance can only indicate an impending breach with the unified space idea formulated by Mies *c.* 1946. In the minuscule plaster scenery of Philip Johnson's guest house the dissolution of such space is rehearsed, is presented as an attractive possibility. On the more solid stage of the St. Louis Airport an operatic realization of related themes makes the possibility more probable and public. Domical vaults, cross vaults, domes in repetition, even folded slabs, all these are obviously means of centralization alternative to the single unique dome. They modulate the section of the building, introduce concavities, plough up the roof slab, animate the space beneath, and impose a cellular organization upon the plan. They are also themes which were latent in the I.I.T. Administration and Library Building. They are among the logical conclusions of the compartmentalizing of space which was there intimated; and, as representing the vertical stressing of space, they are among the possibilities which, for himself, Mies apparently felt obliged to reject.

One might, of course, detect in all these maneuvers the hankering for a Beaux Arts spatial system, for something reassuringly familiar and yet modern, for something comfortably womblike and yet seeming to belong to the future. But, rather than proceed in this way, it might be best, if the Library and Administration Building is indeed a critical project which seems to point in a variety of directions, to direct attention to what seems to be the most logical and daring *dénouement* of what was there implied.

Louis Kahn's project for a Jewish Community Center (Figures 16, 17) at Trenton, New Jersey, with its arches and brick piers, could be regarded as a self-consciously primitivistic version of a Beaux Arts proposal. It may not be dependent on Mies's Library and Administration Building and there is no reason to suppose that it is; but both of these schemes, at least, do display an analogous *parti.* The one shows a library and offices, the other a gymnasium and meeting rooms; but both sets of accommodation are assembled within rectangular blocks of comparable proportion and each block is susceptible to similar courtyard penetrations and to a variety of entrances. Also, about each building there is something a little

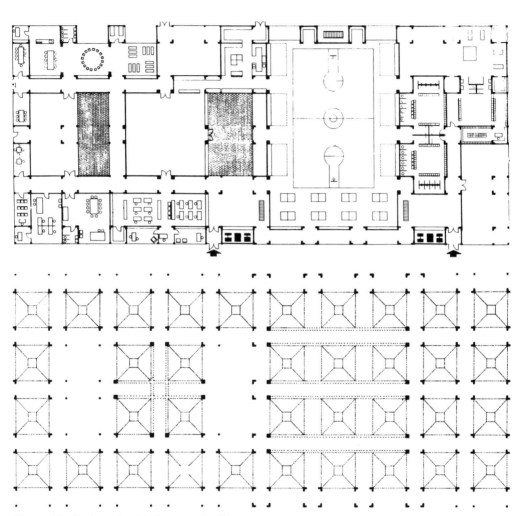

Figure 16   Project, Jewish Community Center, Trenton, N.J. Louis Kahn, 1956- .

Figure 17   Jewish Community Center. Reflected ceiling plan.

heroic and a little strained. They are, both of them, more than interesting but a little less than plausible; both of them clever buildings but not quite conclusive ones; and something of their quality no doubt derives, in each case, from their architect's quite insistent determination to jam discrete functions within the same volume. But then there is more than this. Kahn, apparently, does not feel Mies's scruples with reference to an elegant structure. He is willing to tolerate an inflated structure and one which, by technological criteria, could be criticized as arbitrary and retarded. Thus, he can augment Mies's columns and equip them with mass so that they articulate rather than probe space; similarly, in the place of Mies's flat slab, he can engender a whole colony of pyramids; and, by these means, he is able to take up what the Mies project seems to infer but what an understandable inhibition prevented Mies himself from pursuing. That is, Kahn is able to accept the pressure of structure upon space; and, in doing so, by frankly accepting the existence of minor points of central emphasis and individuated spatiostructural cells, he can then proceed to make a building out of just these, a building which becomes firm and palpable in precisely those situations where the Miesian example remains delicate and tentative.

Now, whether this is gain or loss will, up to a point, be a matter of taste. Over something like the Library and Administration Building Kahn lays a complex grid of maybe Wrightian, maybe Beaux Arts origin; and this grid gives to his project something of that Scotch plaid quality which is as characteristic of Blenheim Palace as it is of the Martin House at Buffalo as it is of so many Prix de Rome. It gives an internal substance and animation to his proposal which enables it to stand up to the outer world in a manner that the Library and Administration Building scarcely can. But, while the evidence of such apparatus as this could suggest, rightly or wrongly, that Kahn is interested in proceeding in a direction where Mies has feared to tread, it might still be not impertinent to introduce some observations.

Whether dependent or not upon the precedent of the Library and Administration Building, the Jewish Community Center is emphatically the most complete development to date of themes which were there scarcely allowed to surface; and, compared with the other neo-'Classical' manifestations which we have examined, it seems so far to present the most comprehensive solution to the problems initiated by the anxiety to introduce centralization and/or the vertical stressing of space. But one might still ask exactly what has been gained by this solution; and certainly there has been scarcely a gain in flexibility. For, if there is a quality of sclerosis in late Mies, there is something equally sclerotic in this proposal for Trenton. In the one case there is an obsession with the flat slab, in the other with pyramids; but, while both obsessions do control and order, neither the flat slab nor the colony of pyramids can be said to answer very conspicuously to what is going on beneath them. With Mies the flat slab rejects the episodes which the columniation acts to sponsor, with Kahn the pyramids propose episodes in plan which only rarely receive a corresponding recognition; and, if one may very well prefer the staccato and aggressiveness of Kahn's pyramids, the inward and outward show of his building, to the apparent Miesian indecision, it is still necessary to ask to what general conclusion such a proposal as his might lead.

Very briefly, it might be suggested that Mies van der Rohe's specific propositions, like Le Corbusier's—though not to so extreme a degree—derive from certain general suppositions as to the nature of the building process and the nature of society. It might, therefore, be proposed that a building by Mies, like a building by Le Corbusier, whether successful or not, is always a statement about the world and never simply a statement about itself. And, in addition, it may be insisted that, for all the ideality of their positions, both Mies and Le Corbusier subscribe to what must be considered fact, that they both of them recognize and accept what is surely the normative condition of twentieth century building—the flat slab and its point supports.

Now it is difficult to see how there can be any evasion of this situation, how in a multistoried building, whether residential or commercial, so long as floors remain horizontal, the slab can be puckered; and it is therefore difficult to see how, in the normative building, there can be opportunity for those vertical stresses which seem, at present, so much to be desired. Domes, pyramids, etc., will permit and encourage vertical stress; but, in the typical scene, these can only rarely be incorporated. Structure, or its expression, may also be so distorted that a frame building can be presented as, seemingly, an accumulation of pavilions; but, again, in doing so the notions of the normative and typical are just as seriously breached. And it is, therefore, both the failure to observe a basic datum and the absence of typicality (that most classical of classical requirements) which must be insisted upon in any evaluation of the adequacy of the classicizing propositions which have here been discussed.

For the most part, perhaps, these buildings should be regarded as interesting aberrations which are relative to private rather than to public problems; and, if their individual merits may sometimes be considerable, it is just possible that they should be regarded as protests against a situation rather than, in themselves, as sponsoring one. And this predicament could allow for irony. For surely, in rejecting the free plan (or International Style space) these classicizing movements, whether consciously or otherwise, have rejected the greatest and most remarkable discovery of twentieth century architecture, something enormously difficult to manage but also something immensely rewarding when successfully manipulated.

But, if the rejection of the free plan may seem to be regressive and based upon insufficient information, then we may also be faced with a more complex reason for irony. For it has been emphasized that there is another and more legitimate form of 'regression' which the classicizing mutations under discussion infer. It has been suggested that, at least in part, these derive from the rejection of the notion of an overriding, coercive, and creative *zeitgeist*; and, if this could indeed be the case, then, whatever its provincial failings, the initial intention of neo-'Classicism' should surely deserve some recognition.

Notes

1 Philip Johnson, *Mies van der Rohe*, New York, 1947, p. 194.

2 Louis Sullivan, *Autobiography of an Idea*, New York, 1924.

3 Le Corbusier and Pierre Jeanneret, *Oeuvre complète 1910-1929*, 3rd ed., Zurich, 1943, p. 129.

4 Henry Adams, *The Education of Henry Adams*, Boston and New York, 1918, p. 455.

Plate 56   Crown Hall, Chicago. Mies van der
Rohe, 1956.

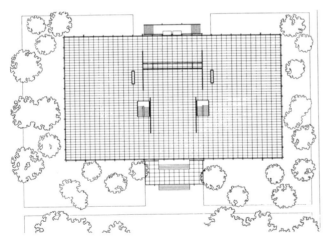

Plate 57   Project, Drive-in Restaurant. Mies
van der Rohe, 1946.

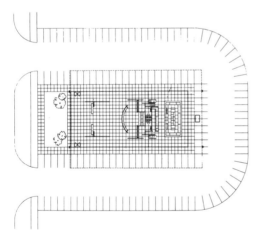

Transparency: Literal
and Phenomenal
(with Robert Slutzky)

Written, 1955-6. First published in
*Perspecta*, 1963. Reprinted as *Transparenz*,
B. Hoesli, ed., Birkhäser, Basel, 1968.

*Transparency* 1591   1. The quality or condition of being transparent; diaphen-
eity; pellucidity 1615. 2. That which is transparent 1591. b. *spec.* A picture,
print, inscription or device on some translucent substance, made visible by means
of light behind 1807. c. A photograph or picture on glass or other transparent
substance intended to be seen by transmitted light 1874. 3. A burlesque translation of the German title of address *Durchlaucht* 1844.

*Transparent*   1. Having the property of transmitting light, so as to render bodies
lying beyond completely visible, that can be seen through. b. Penetrating, as light
1593. c. Admitting the passage of light through interstices (*rare*) 1693. 2. *fig.*
a. Open, candid, ingenuous 1590. b. Easily seen through, recognized, or detected;
manifest, obvious 1592.

'Simultaneity,' 'interpenetration,' 'superimposition,' 'ambivalence,' 'space-time,'
'transparency': in the literature of contemporary architecture these words, and
others like them, are often used as synonyms. We are all familiar with the manifestations to which they are applied—or assume ourselves to be so. These are, we
believe, the specific formal characteristics of contemporary architecture; and, as
we respond to these, we rarely seek to analyze the nature of our response.

It may indeed be futile to attempt to make efficient critical instruments of such
approximate definitions. Perhaps any such attempt can only result in sophistries.
Yet it also becomes evident that, unless the evasive nature of these words is examined, we could be in danger of misinterpreting the forms of lucid complexity
to which they may sometimes refer; and it is for this reason that here some attempt will be made to expose certain levels of meaning with which the term
'transparency' has become endowed.

By the dictionary definition the quality or state of being transparent is a material condition—that of being pervious to light and air, the result of an intellectual
imperative—of our inherent demand for that which should be easily detected,
perfectly evident; and an attribute of personality—the absence of guile, pretence
or dissimulation; and thus the adjective transparent, by defining a purely physical
significance, by functioning as a critical honorific, and in being dignified by far
from disagreeable moral overtones, is a word, from the first, richly loaded with
the possibilities of both meaning and misunderstanding.

But, in addition to these accepted connotations, as a condition to be discovered
in a work of art, transparency has become involved with further levels of interpretation which, in his *Language of Vision*, are admirably defined by Gyorgy Kepes:

If one sees two or more figures overlapping one another, and each of them claims
for itself the common overlapped part, then one is confronted with a contradiction of spatial dimensions. To resolve this contradiction one must assume the

presence of a new optical quality. The figures are endowed with transparency: that is, they are able to interpenetrate without an optical destruction of each other. Transparency however implies more than an optical characteristic, it implies a broader spatial order. Transparency means a simultaneous perception of different spatial locations. Space not only recedes but fluctuates in a continuous activity. The position of the transparent figures has equivocal meaning as one sees each figure now as the closer, now as the further one.[1]

Thus, there is now introduced a conception of transparency quite distinct from any physical quality of substance and almost equally remote from the idea of the transparent as the perfectly clear. In fact, by this definition, the transparent ceases to be that which is perfectly clear and becomes, instead, that which is clearly ambiguous. Nor is this definition an entirely esoteric one; and when we read (as we so often do) of 'transparent overlapping planes' we sense that more than a physical transparency is involved.

For instance, while Moholy-Nagy in his *Vision in Motion* constantly refers to "transparent cellophane sheets," "transparent plastic," "transparency and moving light," "Rubens' radiant transparent shadows,"[2] a careful reading of the book might suggest that for him such literal transparency is often furnished with certain metaphorical qualities. Some superimpositions of form, Moholy tells us, "overcome space and time fixations. They transpose insignificant singularities into meaningful complexities . . . The transparent qualities of the superimpositions often suggest transparency of context as well, revealing unnoticed structural qualities in the object."[3] And again, in commenting on what he calls "the manifold word agglutinations" of James Joyce, on the Joycean 'pun,' Moholy finds that these are "the approach to the practical task of building up a completeness by an ingenious transparency of relationships."[4] In other words, he seems to have felt that, by a process of distortion, recomposition, and *double entendre*, a linguistic transparency—the literary equivalent of Kepes' "interpenetration without optical destruction"—might be effected and that whoever experiences one of these Joycean 'agglutinations' will enjoy the sensation of looking through a first plane of significance to others lying behind.

Therefore, at the beginning of any inquiry into transparency, a basic distinction must perhaps be established. Transparency may be an inherent quality of substance—as in a wire mesh or glass curtain wall, or it may be an inherent quality of organization—as both Kepes and, to a lesser degree, Moholy suggest it to be; and one might, for this reason, distinguish between a real or *literal* and a *phenomenal* or seeming transparency.

Possibly our feeling for literal transparency derives from two sources, from what might be designated as machine aesthetic and from Cubist painting; probably our feeling for phenomenal transparency derives from Cubist painting alone; and, certainly any Cubist canvas of 1911-12 could serve to illustrate the presence of these two orders or levels of the transparent.

But, in considering phenomena so baffling and complex as those which distinguish Cubist painting, the would-be analyst is at a disadvantage; and, presumably, it is for this reason that, almost fifty years after the event, dispassionate analysis of the Cubist achievement is still almost entirely lacking.[5] Explanations which obscure the pictorial problems of Cubism are to be found in abundance, and one might be sceptical of these, just as one might be sceptical of those two plausible interpretations which involve the fusion of temporal and spatial factors, which see Cubism as a premonition of relativity, and which in this way present it as little more than a 'natural' by-product of a particular cultural atmosphere. As Alfred Barr tells us, Apollinaire "invoked the fourth dimension . . . in a metaphorical rather than a mathematical sense";[6] and, rather than attempt to relate Picasso to Minkowski, it would, for us, be preferable to refer to less disputable sources of inspiration.

A late Cézanne such as the *Mont Sainte Victoire* of 1904-6 (Plate 58) in the Philadelphia Museum of Art is characterized by certain extreme simplifications: most notably, by a highly developed insistence on a frontal viewpoint of the whole scene; by a suppression of the more obvious elements suggestive of depth; and by a resultant contracting of foreground, middleground, and background into a distinctly compressed pictorial matrix. Sources of light are definite but various; and a further contemplation of the picture reveals a tipping forward of the objects in space, which is assisted by the painter's use of opaque and contrasted color and made more emphatic by the intersection of the canvas provided by the base of the mountain. The center of the composition is occupied by a rather dense gridding of oblique and rectilinear lines; and this area is then buttressed and stabilized by a more insistent horizontal and vertical grid which introduces a certain peripheric interest.

Frontality, suppression of depth, contracting of space, definition of light sources, tipping forward of objects, restricted palette, oblique and rectilinear grids, propensities towards peripheric development, are all characteristics of Analytical Cubism; and, in the typical compositions of 1911-12, detached from a more overtly representational purpose, they assume a more evident significance. In these pictures, apart from the pulling to pieces and reassembly of objects, perhaps above all we are conscious of a further shrinkage of depth and an increased emphasis which is now awarded to the grid. We discover about this time a meshing of two systems of coordinates. On the one hand an arrangement of oblique and curved lines suggests a certain diagonal spatial recession. On the other, a series of horizontal and vertical lines implies a contradictory statement of frontality. Generally speaking, the oblique and curved lines possess a certain naturalistic significance while the rectilinear ones show a geometricizing tendency serving as a reassertion of the picture plane. But both systems of coordinates provide for the orientation of the figures simultaneously in an extended space and on a painted surface, while their intersecting, overlapping, interlocking, their building up into larger and fluctuating configurations, permits the genesis of the typical Cubist motif.

But, as the observer distinguishes between all the planes to which these grids give rise, he becomes progressively conscious of an opposition between certain areas of luminous paint and others of a more dense coloration. He distinguishes between certain planes to which he is able to attribute a physical nature allied to that of celluloid, others whose essence is semiopaque, and further areas of a substance totally opposed to the transmission of light. And he may discover that all of these planes, translucent or otherwise, and regardless of their representational content, are to be found implicated in the manifestation which Kepes has defined as transparency.

The double nature of this transparency may be illustrated by the comparison and analysis of a somewhat atypical Picasso, *The Clarinet Player* (Plate 59), and a representative Braque, *The Portuguese* (Plate 60), both of 1911. In each picture a pyramidal form implies an image; but then, while Picasso defines his pyramid by means of a strong contour, Braque uses a more complicated inference. Picasso's contour is so assertive and independent of its background that the observer has some sense of a positively transparent figure standing in a relatively deep space, and only subsequently does he redefine this sensation to allow for the real shallowness of the space. But with Braque the reading of the picture follows a reverse order. A highly developed interlacing of horizontal and vertical gridding, created by gapped lines and intruding planes, establishes a primarily shallow space, and only gradually does the observer become able to invest this space with a depth which permits the figure to assume substance. Braque offers the possibility of an independent reading of figure and grid. Picasso scarcely does so. Picasso's grid is rather subsumed within his figure or appears as a form of peripheral incident intended to stabilize it.

The differences of method in these two pictures could easily be overemphasized. At different times they will appear to be dissimilar and alike. But it is necessary to point out that there are present in this parallel the intimations of different directions. In the Picasso we enjoy the sensation of looking through a figure standing in a deep space; whereas in Braque's shallow, flattened, laterally extended space, we are provided with no physically perspicuous object. In the one we receive a prevision of literal, in the other, of phenomenal transparency; and the evidence of these two distinct attitudes will become much clearer if a comparison is attempted between the works of two such slightly later painters as Robert Delaunay and Juan Gris.

Delaunay's *Simultaneous Windows* of 1911 and Gris' *Still Life* of 1912 (Plates 61 and 62) both include objects which are presumably transparent, the one windows, the other bottles; but, while Gris suppresses the literal transparency of glass in favor of a transparency of gridding, Delaunay accepts with unrestrained enthusiasm the elusively reflective qualities of his superimposed 'glazed openings.' Gris weaves a system of oblique and curved lines into some sort of shallow, corrugated space; and, in the architectonic tradition of Cézanne, in order to amplify both his objects and structure, he assumes varied but definite light sources. Delaunay's preoccupation with form presupposes an entirely different attitude. Forms to him—e.g., a low block of buildings and various naturalistic objects reminiscent of the Eiffel Tower—are nothing but reflections and refractions of light which he presents in terms analogous to Cubist gridding. But, despite this geometricizing of image, the generally ethereal nature of both Delaunay's forms and his space appears more characteristic of impressionism; and this resemblance is further reinforced by the manner in which he uses his medium. In contrast to the flat, planar areas of opaque and almost monochromatic color which Gris invests with such high tactile value, Delaunay emphasizes a quasi-impressionistic calligraphy; and, while Gris provides explicit definition of a rear plane, Delaunay dissolves the possibilities of so distinct a closure of his space. Gris's rear plane functions as a catalyst which localizes the ambiguities of his pictorial objects and engenders their fluctuating values. Delaunay's distaste for so specific a procedure leaves the latent ambiguities of his form unresolved, exposed, without reference. Both operations might be recognized as attempts to elucidate the congested intricacy of Analytical Cubism; but, where Gris seems to have intensified some of the characteristics of Cubist space and to have imbued its plastic principles with a new bravura, Delaunay has, perhaps, been led to explore the poetical overtones of Cubism by divorcing them from their metrical syntax.

When something of the attitude of a Delaunay becomes fused with a machine-aesthetic emphasis upon materials and stiffened by a certain enthusiasm for planar structures, then literal transparency becomes complete; and perhaps it is most appropriately to be illustrated by the work of Moholy-Nagy. In his *Abstract of an Artist*, Moholy tells us that around 1921 his "transparent paintings" became completely freed from all elements reminiscent of nature, and, to quote him directly, "I see today that this was the logical result of the Cubist paintings which I had admiringly studied."[7]

Now whether a freedom from all elements reminiscent of nature may be considered a logical continuation of Cubism is not relevant to the present discussion, but whether Moholy did succeed in emptying his work of all naturalistic content is of some importance; and his seeming belief that Cubism had pointed the way towards a freeing of forms may justify us in the analysis of one of his subsequent works and its parallel with another post-Cubist painting. With Moholy's *La Sarraz* of 1930 (Plate 63) might reasonably be compared a Fernand Léger of 1926, *Three Faces* (Plate 64).

In *La Sarraz* five circles connected by an S-shaped band, two sets of trapezoidal planes of translucent color, a number of near horizontal and vertical bars, a liberal splattering of light and dark flecks, and a number of slightly convergent dashes are all imposed upon a black background. In *Three Faces* three major areas displaying organic forms, abstracted artifacts, and purely geometric shapes are tied together by horizontal banding and common contour. In contrast to Moholy, Léger aligns his pictorial objects at right angles to each other and to the edges of his picture plane; he provides these objects with a flat, opaque coloring, setting up a figure-ground reading through the compressed disposition of highly contrasted surfaces; and, while Moholy seems to have flung open a window on to some private version of outer space, Léger, working within an almost two-dimensional scheme, achieves a maximum clarity of both 'negative' and 'positive' forms. By means of restriction, Léger's picture becomes charged with an equivocal depth reading, with a phenomenal transparency singularly reminiscent of that to which Moholy was so sensitive in the writings of Joyce, but which, in spite of the literal transparency of his paint, he himself has been unable or unwilling to achieve.

For, in spite of its modernity of motif, Moholy's picture still shows the conventional pre-Cubist foreground, middleground and background; and, in spite of a rather casual interweaving of surface and depth elements introduced to destroy the logic of this deep space, Moholy's picture can be submitted to only one reading. But the case of Léger is very different. For Léger, through the refined virtuosity with which he assembles post-Cubist constituents, makes completely plain the multifunctioned behavior of clearly defined form. Through flat planes, through an absence of volume suggesting its presence, through the implication rather than the fact of a grid, through an interrupted checkerboard pattern stimulated by color, proximity, and discreet superimposition, he leads the eye to experience an inexhaustible series of larger and smaller organizations within the whole. Léger's concern is with the structure of form: Moholy's with materials and light. Moholy has accepted the Cubist figure but has lifted it from out of its spatial matrix: Léger has preserved and even intensified the typically Cubist tension between figure and space.

These three comparisons may clarify some of the basic differences between literal and phenomenal transparency in the painting of the last forty-five years. Literal transparency, we might notice, tends to be associated with the *trompe l'oeil* effect of a translucent object in a deep, naturalistic space; while phenomenal transparency seems to be found when a painter seeks the articulated presentation of frontally aligned objects in a shallow, abstracted space.

But, in considering architectural rather than pictorial transparencies, inevitable confusions arise. For, while painting can only imply the third dimension, architecture cannot suppress it. Provided with the reality rather than the counterfeit of three dimensions, in architecture, literal transparency can become a physical fact; but phenomenal transparency will be more difficult to achieve—and is, indeed, so difficult to discuss that generally critics have been entirely willing to associate transparency in architecture exclusively with a transparency of materials. Thus Gyorgy Kepes, having provided an almost classical explanation of the phenomena we have noticed in Braque, Gris, and Léger, appears to consider that the architectural analogue of these must be found in the physical qualities of glass and plastics, that the equivalent of carefully calculated Cubist and post-Cubist compositions will be discovered in the haphazard superimpositions provided by the accidental reflections of light playing upon a translucent or polished surface.[8] And, similarly, Siegfried Giedion seems to assume that the presence of an all-glass wall at the Bauhaus (Plate 65), with "its extensive transparent areas," permits "the hovering relations of planes and the kind of 'overlapping' which appears in contemporary painting"; and he proceeds to reinforce this suggestion with a quotation from Alfred Barr on the characteristic "transparency of overlapping planes" in analytical Cubism.[9]

In Picasso's *L'Arlésienne* (Plate 66), the picture which provides the visual support for these inferences of Giedion's, such a transparency of overlapping planes is very obviously to be found. There Picasso offers planes apparently of celluloid through which the observer has the sensation of looking; and, in doing so, no doubt his sensations are somewhat similar to those of an observer of the workshop wing at the Bauhaus. In each case a transparency of materials is discovered. But then, in the laterally constructed space of his picture, Picasso, through the compilation of larger and smaller forms, also offers limitless possibilities of alternative interpretation. *L'Arlésienne* has the fluctuating, equivocal meaning which Kepes recognizes as characteristic of transparency; while the glass wall at the Bauhaus, an unambiguous surface giving upon an unambiguous space, seems to be singularly free of this quality; and thus, for the evidence of what we have designated phenomenal transparency, we shall here be obliged to look elsewhere.

Almost contemporary with the Bauhaus, Le Corbusier's villa at Garches (Plates 5 and 6) might fairly be juxtaposed with it. Superficially, the garden facade of this house and the elevations of the workshop wing at the Bauhaus (Plate 67) are not dissimilar. Both employ cantilevered wall slabs and both display a recessed ground floor. Neither admits an interruption of the horizontal movement of the glazing and both make a point of carrying this glazing around the corner. But further similarities are looked for in vain. From here on, one might say that Le Corbusier is primarily occupied with the planar qualities of glass and Gropius with its translucent attributes. By the introduction of a wall surface almost equal in height to that of his glazing divisions, Le Corbusier stiffens his glass plane and provides it with an overall surface tension; while Gropius permits his translucent surface the appearance of hanging rather loosely from a fascia which protrudes somewhat in the fashion of a curtain box. At Garches one may enjoy the illusion that *possibly* the framing of the windows passes behind the wall surface; but, at the Bauhaus, since one is never for a moment unaware that the slab is pressing up behind the window, one is not enabled to indulge in such speculations.

At Garches the ground floor is conceived of as a vertical surface traversed by a range of horizontal windows; at the Bauhaus it is given the appearance of a solid wall extensively punctured by glazing. At Garches it offers an explicit indication of the frame which carries the cantilevers above; at the Bauhaus it shows somewhat stubby piers which do not automatically connect with the idea of a skeleton structure. In this workshop wing of the Bauhaus one might say that Gropius is absorbed with the idea of establishing a plinth upon which to dispose an arrangement of horizontal planes, and that his principal concern appears to be the wish that two of these planes should be visible through a veil of glass. But glass would hardly seem to hold such fascination for Le Corbusier; and, although one can obviously see through his windows, it is not here that the transparency of his building is to be found.

At Garches (Plate 10) the recessed surface of the ground floor is redefined upon the roof by the two free-standing walls which terminate the terrace; and the same statement of depth is taken up by the glazed doors in the side walls which act as conclusions to the fenestration (Plate 7). In these ways Le Corbusier proposes the idea that, immediately behind his glazing, there lies a narrow slot of space traveling parallel to it; and, of course, in consequence of this, he implies a further idea— that bounding this slot of space, and behind it, there lies a plane of which the ground floor, the free-standing walls, and the inner reveals of the doors all form a part; and, although this plane may be dismissed as very obviously a conceptual convenience rather than a physical fact, its obtrusive presence is undeniable. Recognizing the physical plane of glass and concrete and this imaginary (though scarcely less real) plane that lies behind, we become aware that here a transparency is effected not through the agency of a window but rather through our being made conscious of primary concepts which "interpenetrate without optical destruction of each other."

And obviously these two planes are not all, since a third and equally distinct parallel surface is both introduced and implied. It defines the rear wall of the terrace, and is further reiterated by other parallel dimensions: the parapets of the garden stairs, the terrace, and the second-floor balcony. In itself, each of these planes is incomplete or perhaps even fragmentary; yet it is with these parallel planes as points of reference that the facade is organized, and the implication of all is that of a vertical layerlike stratification of the interior space of the building, of a succession of laterally extended spaces traveling one behind the other.

It is this system of spatial stratification which brings Le Corbusier's facade into the closest relationship with the Léger we have already examined. In *Three Faces* Léger conceives of his canvas as a field modeled in low relief. Of his three major panels (which overlap, dovetail, and alternately comprise and exclude each other), two are closely implicated in an almost equivalent depth relationship, while the third constitutes a *coulisse* which both advances and recedes. At Garches, Le Corbusier replaces Léger's picture plane with a most highly developed regard for the frontal viewpoint (the preferred views include only the slightest deviations from parallel perspective); Léger's canvas becomes Le Corbusier's second plane; other planes are either imposed upon or subtracted from this basic datum; and deep space is then contrived in similar *coulisse* fashion, with the facade cut open and depth inserted into the ensuing slot.

These remarks, which might infer that Le Corbusier had indeed succeeded in alienating architecture from its necessary three-dimensional existence, require qualification; and, in order to provide it, it is now necessary to proceed to some discussion of the building's internal space. And here, at the very beginning, it may be noticed that this space appears to be a flat contradiction of the facade, particularly on the principal floor (Plate 7) where the volume revealed is almost directly opposite to that which might have been anticipated. Thus, the glazing of the garden facade might have suggested the presence of a single large room behind it; and it might have further inspired the belief that the direction of this room was parallel with that of the facade. But the internal divisions of the space deny any such statement, disclosing, instead, a major volume whose primary direction is at right angles to the facade; while, in both the major volume and in the subsidiary spaces which surround it, the predominance of this direction is further conspicuously emphasized by the flanking walls.

But the spatial structure of this floor is obviously more complex than at first appears, and ultimately it compels a revision of these initial assumptions. Gradually the lateral nature of the cantilevered slots becomes evident; and, while the apse of the dining room, the position of the principal stairs, the void, the library, all reaffirm the same dimension, by means of these elements the planes of the facade can now be seen to effect a profound modification of the deep extension of the internal space, which now comes to approach the stratified succession of flattened spaces suggested by the external appearance.

So much might be said for a reading of the internal volumes in terms of the vertical planes; and a further reading in terms of the horizontal planes, the floors, will reveal similar characteristics. Thus, after recognizing that a floor is not a wall and that plans are not paintings, we might still examine these horizontal planes in very much the same manner as we have the facade, again selecting *Three Faces* as a point of departure. A complement of Léger's picture plane may now be offered by the roofs of the penthouse and the elliptical pavilion, by the summits of the free-standing walls and by the top of the rather curious gazebo—all of which lie on the same surface (Plate 10). The second plane now becomes the major roof terrace and the *coulisse* space becomes the cut in the slab which leads the eye down to the terrace below; and similar parallels are very obvious in considering the organization of the principal floor. For here the vertical equivalent of deep space is introduced by the double height of the outer terrace and by the void connecting living room with entrance hall; and here, just as Léger enlarges spatial dimensions through the displacement of the inner edges of his outer panels, so Le Corbusier encroaches upon the space of his central area.

Thus, throughout this house, there is that contradiction of spatial dimensions which Kepes recognizes as characteristic of transparency. There is a continuous dialectic between fact and implication. The reality of deep space is constantly opposed to the inference of shallow; and, by means of the resultant tension, reading after reading is enforced. The five layers of space which, vertically, divide the building's volume and the four layers which cut it horizontally will all, from time to time, claim attention; and this gridding of space will then result in continuous fluctuations of interpretation.

These possibly cerebral refinements are scarcely so conspicuous at the Bauhaus; indeed they are attributes of which an aesthetic of materials is apt to be impatient. In the workshop wing of the Bauhaus it is the literal transparency which Giedion has chiefly applauded, at Garches it is the phenomenal transparency which has engaged our attention; and, if with some reason we have been able to relate the achievement of Le Corbusier to that of Léger, with equal justification we might notice a community of interest in the expression of Gropius and Moholy.

Moholy was always preoccupied with the expression of glass, metal, reflecting substances, light; and Gropius, at least in the 1920s, would seem to have been equally concerned with the idea of using materials for their intrinsic qualities. Both, it may be said without injustice, received a certain stimulus from the experiments of *De Stijl* and the Russian Constructivists; but both apparently were unwilling to accept certain more Parisian conclusions.

For, seemingly, it was in Paris that the Cubist 'discovery' of shallow space was most completely exploited; and it was there that the idea of the picture plane as uniformly activated field was most entirely understood. With Picasso, Braque, Gris, Léger, Ozenfant, we are never conscious of the picture plane functioning in any passive role. Both it, as negative space, and the objects placed upon it, as positive figure, are endowed with an equal capacity to stimulate. But outside the school of Paris this condition is not typical, although Mondrian, a Parisian by adoption, constitutes one major exception and Klee another. But a glance at any representative works of Kandinsky, Malevitch, El Lissitzky, or Van Doesburg will reveal that these painters, like Moholy, scarcely felt the necessity of providing any distinct spatial matrix for their principal objects. They are apt to accept a simplification of the Cubist image as a composition of geometrical planes, but they are apt to reject the comparable Cubist abstraction of space; and, if for these reasons their pictures offer us figures which float in an infinite, atmospheric, naturalistic void, without any of the rich Parisian stratification of volume, the Bauhaus may be accepted as their architectural equivalent.

Thus, in the Bauhaus complex, although we are presented with a composition of slablike buildings whose forms suggest the possibility of a reading of space by layers, we are scarcely conscious of the presence of spatial stratification. Through the movements of the dormitory building, the administrative offices, and the workshop wing, the principal floor may suggest a channeling of space in one direction (Figure 18). Through the countermovements of roadway, classrooms, and auditorium wing, the ground floor may suggest a movement of space in the other (Figure 19). A preference for neither direction is stated; and the ensuing dilemma is resolved, as indeed it only can be resolved in this case, by giving priority to diagonal points of view.

Much as Van Doesburg and Moholy eschew Cubist frontality, so does Gropius; and it is significant that, while the published photographs of Garches tend to minimize factors of diagonal recession, almost invariably the published photographs of the Bauhaus tend to play up just these factors. And the importance of these diagonal views of the Bauhaus is constantly reasserted—by the translucent corner of the workshop wing and by such features as the balconies of the dormitory and the protruding slab over the entrance to the workshops, features which require for their understanding a renunciation of the principle of frontality.

In plan, the Bauhaus reveals a succession of spaces but scarcely 'a contradiction of spatial dimensions.' Relying on the diagonal viewpoint, Gropius has exteriorized the opposed movements of his space, has allowed them to flow away into infinity; and, by being unwilling to attribute to either one any significant difference of quality, he has prohibited the possibilities of a potential ambiguity. Thus, only the contours of his buildings assume a layerlike character; but these layers of building scarcely act to suggest a layerlike structure of either internal or external space. Denied, by these means, the possibility of penetrating a stratified space defined either by real planes or their imaginary projections, the observer is also denied the possibility of experiencing those conflicts between one space which is explicit and another which is implied. He may enjoy the sensation of looking through a glass wall and thus be able to see the interior and the exterior of the building simultaneously; but, in doing so, he will be conscious of few of those equivocal emotions which derive from phenomenal transparency.

But to some degree, since the one is a single block and the other a complex of wings, an extended comparison between Garches and the Bauhaus is unjust to both. For, within the limitations of a simple volume, it is possible that certain relationships can be inferred which, in a more elaborate composition, will always lie beyond the bounds of possibility; and, for these reasons, it may be more apt to distinguish literal from phenomenal transparency by a further parallel between Gropius and Le Corbusier.

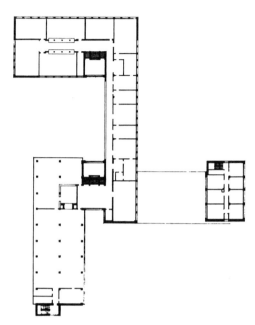

Figure 18   Bauhaus, Dessau. Plan of principal floor. Walter Gropius, 1925-26.

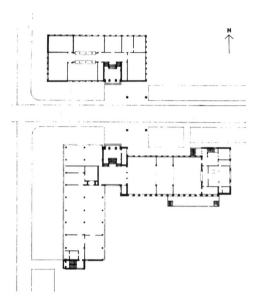

Figure 19   Bauhaus, Dessau. Plan of ground floor.

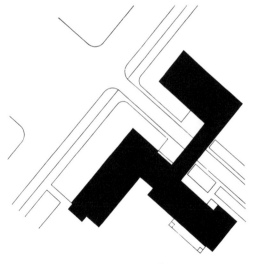

Figure 20   Bauhaus, Dessau. Plan.

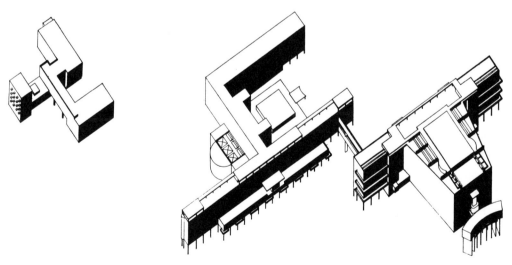

Figure 21   Bauhaus and Palace of the League
of Nations. Axonometrics.

Le Corbusier's League of Nations project of 1927 (Plates 68 and 69), like the Bauhaus, possesses heterogeneous elements and functions which lead to an extended organization and to the appearance of a further feature which both buildings have in common: the narrow block. But it is here again that similarities cease: for, while the Bauhaus blocks pinwheel in a manner highly suggestive of Constructivist compositions (Figure 20), in the League of Nations these same long blocks define a system of striations almost more rigid than is evident at Garches.

In the League of Nations project lateral extension characterizes the two principal wings of the Secretariat, qualifies the library and book stack area, is reemphasized by the entrance quay and foyers of the General Assembly Building, and dominates even the auditorium itself. There, the introduction of glazing along the side walls, disturbing the normal focus of the hall upon the presidential box, introduces the same transverse direction. And, by such means, the counterstatement of deep space becomes a highly assertive proposition, chiefly suggested by a lozenge shape whose major axis passes through the General Assembly Building and whose outline is comprised by a mirror image projection of the auditorium volume into the approach roads of the *cour d'honneur*. But again, as at Garches, the intimations of depth inherent in this form are consistently retracted. A cut, a displacement, and a sliding sideways occur along the line of its minor axis; and, as a figure, it is repeatedly scored through and broken down into a series of lateral references—by trees, by circulations, by the momentum of the buildings themselves—so that finally, by a series of positive and negative implications, the whole area becomes a sort of monumental debate, an argument between a real and deep space and an ideal and shallow one.

We will presume the Palace of the League of Nations as having been built and an observer following the axial approach to its auditorium. Necessarily he is subjected to the polar attraction of its principal entrance which he sees framed within a screen of trees. But these trees, intersecting his vision, also introduce a lateral deflection of interest, so that he becomes successively aware, first, of a relation between the flanking office building and the foreground *parterre*, and second, of a relation between the crosswalk and the courtyard of the Secretariat. And once within the trees, beneath the low umbrella which they provide, yet a further tension is established: the space, which is inflected towards the General Assembly Building, is defined by, and reads as, a projection of the book stack and library. And finally, with the trees as a volume behind him, the observer at last finds himself standing on a low terrace, confronting the entrance quay but separated from it by a rift of space so complete that it is only by the propulsive power of the walk behind him that he can be enabled to cross it. With his arc of vision no longer restricted, he is now offered the General Assembly Building in its full extent; but since a newly revealed lack of focus compels his eye to slide along this facade, it is again irresistibly drawn sideways—to the view of gardens and lake beyond. And should the observer turn around from this rift between him and his obvious goal, and should he look back at the trees which he has just abandoned, he will find that the lateral sliding of the space becomes only more determined, emphasized by the trees themselves and the cross alley leading into the slotted indenture alongside the bookstack. While further, if our observer is a man of moderate sophistication, and if the piercing of a volume or screen of trees by a road might have come to suggest to him that the intrinsic function of this road is to penetrate similar volumes and screens, then, by inference, the terrace upon which he is standing becomes, not a prelude to the auditorium, as its axial relationship suggests, but a projection of the volumes and planes of the office building with which it is aligned.

These stratifications, devices by means of which space becomes constructed, substantial, and articulate, are the essence of that phenomenal transparency which has been noticed as characteristic of the central post-Cubist tradition. They have never been noticed as characteristic of the Bauhaus. For obviously there completely different space conceptions are manifest. In the League of Nations project Le Corbusier provides the observer with a series of quite specific locations: at the Bauhaus the observer is without such points of reference. Although the League of Nations project is extensively glazed, except in the auditorium, such glazing is scarcely of capital importance. At the Palace of the League of Nations corners and angles, as the indices of spatial dimension, are assertive and definite. At the Bauhaus, Giedion tells us, they are "dematerialized." At the Palace of the League of Nations space is crystalline; but at the Bauhaus it is glazing which gives the building a "crystalline translucence." At the Palace of the League of Nations glass provides a surface as definite and as taut as the top of a drum; but at the Bauhaus glass walls "flow into one another," "blend into each other," "wrap around the building," and in other ways (by acting as the absence of plane) "contribute to that process of loosening up which now dominates the architectural scene."[10]

But we look in vain for 'loosening up' in the Palace of the League of Nations. There is no evidence there of any desire to obliterate sharp distinction. Le Corbusier's planes are like knives for the apportionate slicing of space. If we could attribute to space the qualities of water, then his building is like a dam by means of which space is contained, embanked, tunneled, sluiced, and finally spilled into the informal gardens alongside the lake. While by contrast, the Bauhaus, insulated in a sea of amorphic outline, is like a reef gently lapped by a placid tide (Figure 21).

The foregoing, no doubt an overextended discussion of two schemes, the one mutilated, the other unbuilt, has been a necessary means towards clarifying the spatial milieu in which phenomenal transparency becomes possible. It is not intended to suggest that phenomenal transparency (for all its Cubist descent) is a necessary constituent of modern architecture, nor that its presence might be used as a piece of litmus paper for the test of architectural orthodoxy. It is simply intended to serve as a characterization of species and, also, as a warning against the confusion of species.

## Notes

1 Gyorgy Kepes, *Language of Vision*, Chicago, 1944, p. 77.

2 László Moholy-Nagy, *Vision in Motion*, Chicago, 1947; pp. 188, 194, 159, 157.

3 *Ibid.*, p. 210.

4 *Ibid.*, p. 350.

5 Among these exceptions are to be found studies such as those of Alfred Barr and publications such as Christopher Grey, *Cubist Aesthetic Theory*, Baltimore, 1953, and Winthrop Judkins, "Toward a Reinterpretation of Cubism," *Art Bulletin*, Vol. XXX, No. 4, 1948.

6 Alfred Barr, *Picasso: Fifty Years of His Art*, New York, 1946, p. 68.

7 László Moholy-Nagy, *The New Vision and Abstract of an Artist*, New York, 1947, p. 75.

8 Kepes, pp. 79, 117 and elsewhere.

9 Siegfried Giedion, *Space, Time and Architecture*, Cambridge, Mass., ed. 1954, pp. 490, and 491.

10 *Ibid.*, p. 489, and Siegfried Giedion, *Walter Gropius*, New York, 1954, pp. 54-55.

Plate 58   Paul Cézanne, *Mont Sainte Victoire*,
1904-6.

Plate 59   Pablo Picasso, *The Clarinet Player*, 1911.

Plate 60   Georges Braque, *The Portuguese*, 1911.

Plate 61   Robert Delaunay, *Simultaneous Windows*, 1911.

Plate 62   Juan Gris, *Still Life*, 1912.

Plate 63   László Moholy-Nagy, *La Sarraz*, 1930.

Plate 64   Fernand Léger, *Three Faces*, 1926.

Plate 65   Bauhaus, Dessau. Walter Gropius, 1925-26.

Plate 66   Picasso, *L'Arlésienne*, 1911-12.

Plate 67    Bauhaus, Dessau. Walter Gropius,
1925-26.

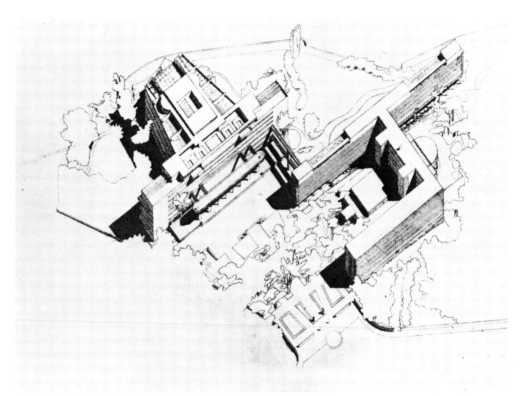

Plate 68   Project. Palace of the League of
Nations, Geneva. Le Corbusier, 1927.

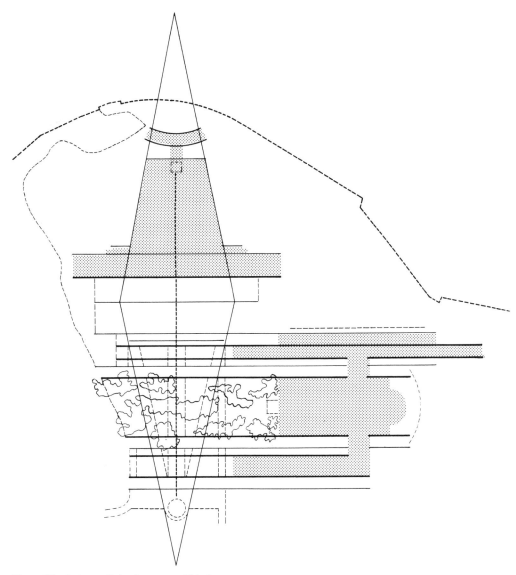

Plate 69   Palace of the League of Nations.
Analytical diagram.

# La Tourette

First published in the *Architectural Review*, 1961, under the title "Dominican Monastery of La Tourette, Eveux-Sur Arbresle, Lyon."

The dimension of depth, whether of space or time, whether visual or aural, always appears in one surface, so that this surface really possesses two values: one when we take it for what it is materially, the other when we see it in its second virtual life. In the latter case the surface, without ceasing to be flat, expands in depth. This is what we call foreshortening. Vision in depth is made possible by foreshortening, in which we find an extreme case of a fusion of simple vision with a purely intellectual act.

—José Ortega y Gasset, *Meditations on Quixote*[1]

In 1916, at La Chaux-de-Fonds, Le Corbusier erected a house with a centrally disposed blank panel (Plate 17). Forty years later, and at a heroic scale, he has repeated something very like this device. At La Chaux-de-Fonds the blank panel is the central figure of a facade. At La Tourette a largely blank wall comprises the north side of the church (Plate 70). But in both cases, in the Villa Schwob and the monastery, as the building is first experienced, the focus of the visual field is provided by a motif without high intrinsic interest; one which, while it absorbs the eye, is unable to retain its attention.

In 1920-21, running through the articles in *L'Esprit nouveau* which were later to be collected as *Vers une architecture*, there appeared the first public evidence of Le Corbusier's intense preoccupation with the Athenian Acropolis:

The apparent disorder of the plan could only deceive the profane. The equilibrium is in no way a paltry one. It is determined by the famous landscape which stretches from the Piraeus to Mount Pentelicus. The plan was conceived to be seen from a distance: the axes follow the valley and the false right angles are constructed with the skill of a first rate stage manager . . . The spectacle is massive, elastic, crushingly acute, dominating . . . The elements of the site rise up like walls panoplied in the power of their cubic coefficient, stratification, material, etc., like the walls of a room . . . The Greeks on the Acropolis set up temples which are animated by a single thought, drawing around them the desolate landscape and drawing it up into the composition.[2]

It is not necessary to continue. But at La Tourette, while Piraeus and Pentelicus are alike lacking; while we are rather presented with a species of Escorial than a type of Parthenon; and while the old château, partly a farmhouse and partly a piece of Second Empire wish-fulfillment, is certainly not the most likely candidate for the role of Propylaea—though differences are so obvious that they need scarcely be stressed—there are still certain patterns of organization, e.g., a compounding of frontal and three-quarter views, an impacting of axial directions, a tension between longitudinal and transverse movements, above all the intersection of an architectonic by a topographical experience—which may, to the initiated, suggest that the spatial mechanics of the monastery's precinct are just possibly some very private commentary upon Acropolitan material.

But the casual visitor to La Tourette will have little conscious time for this precinct. He has climbed a hill, penetrated an archway, and arrived in a graveled courtyard to find himself in what certainly appears to be no more than the picturesque hiatus between two entirely discrete buildings; to be a merely incidental space. To his left there is a mansarded pavilion. It carries a clock with blue Sevres figures. To his right is a kitchen garden of uncertain extent. But these, of which he is dimly aware, are the very subsidiary components of the scene. For right ahead, obsessively prominent and unsupported by any shred of conventional artifice, there is the *machine à émouvoir* which he has come to inspect (Plate 70).

Secretly the casual visitor is a little dismayed. He is no longer to be shocked by the absence of a preface to a work of architecture. He feels that by now he can take any lack of introduction quite in his stride. He is hardened to a very good deal. But he still scarcely expects to be so entirely cold-shouldered as here seems to be the case. A vertical surface gashed by horizontal slots and relieved by a bastion supporting gesticulating entrails; an enigmatic plane which bears, like the injuries of time, the multiple scars which its maker has chosen to inflict upon it; by any standards an inference of his own complete irrelevance—the visitor had anticipated something either a little less or a little more than this. And thus, while the three entrails, the so-called *canons à lumière*, might seem to quiver like the relics of a highly excruciating martyrdom, while the general blankness of the spectacle might seem to be representative of religious anonymity and while a variety of fantasies infiltrate his consciousness, the visitor, since he feels himself to be presented with a random disclosure of the building, is at this stage disinclined to attribute any very great importance to his experience (Plates 71 and 72).

The north side of the church this wall is instinctively known to be. It is doubtful if any other element could be so opaque. So much is evident. But, therefore, while the visitor interprets it frontally, he also attributes to this inscrutable visual barrier the typical behavior patterns of an end elevation. This wall may indeed be a great dam holding back a reservoir of spiritual energy. Such *may* be its symbolical reality. But the visitor also knows it to be part of a building; and he believes himself to be approaching, not this building's front, but its flank. The information which he is being offered, he therefore feels, must be less crucial than simply interesting. The architect is displaying a profile rather than a full face. And, accordingly, since he assumes that the expressive countenance of the building must be around the corner, rather as though the church were the subject of a portrait *en profil perdu*, the visitor now sets out to cross an imaginary picture plane in order to grasp the object in its true frontality.

A certain animation of contour—the oblique cut of the parapet and the intersection with the diagonal of the belfry—will focus his eye and lead him on. But if, for these reasons, the building first insists on rapid approach, as he climbs the hill or moves along the alley within the trees, the visitor is likely to discover that, somehow, this gesture of invitation has vanished and that, the closer he approaches it, the more unsympathetic the building seems to come toward his possible arrival.

This is one aspect of a disconcerting situation; but another should be noticed: that, at a certain stage in the approach route, the building comes to seem utterly drained of importance. For, as one leaves behind the courtyard of the old château, which is the socket of the enclosure in which one had believed oneself to be, one is obliged to exchange a reliable womb for an unpeopled arena. The whole deserted sweep of the upper valley of the Turdine has progressively come into view; the field of experience is transformed, and the nature of the stimuli to which one is subjected becomes systematically more concentrated and ruthless.

Thus, the eye which was previously directed towards the left of the church facade, towards the point of entrance, is now violently dragged away towards the right. The movement of the site has changed. The visual magnet is no longer a wall. Now it has become a horizon. And the wall, which previously acted as backdrop to one field of vision, as a perspective transversal, now operates as a side screen to another, as a major orthogonal which directs attention into the emptiness of the far distance but which, by foiling the foreground incident—the three entrails—also serves to instigate an insupportable tension between the local and the remote. In other words, as the church is approached, the site which had initially seemed so innocent in its behavior becomes a space rifted and ploughed up into almost unbridgable chasms.

This may be to provide too lurid an analysis; but, though it may exaggerate the intensity, it does not seriously distort the quality of an experience which is as unexpected as it is painful. It would be possible, and maybe even justified, to interpret this preliminary *promenade architecturale* as the deliberate implication of a tragic insufficiency in the visitor's status. The wall is exclusive. The visitor may enter, but not on his own terms. The wall is the summation of an institutional program. But the visitor is so placed that he is without the means of making coherent his own experience. He is made the subject of diametric excitations; his consciousness is divided; and, being both deprived of and also offered an architectural support, in order to resolve his predicament, he is anxious, indeed obliged—and without choice—to enter the building.

It is possible, but it is not probable, that all this is uncontrived. However, if one happens to be sceptical of the degree of contrivance, and if one is tempera-

mentally predisposed to consider the game of hunt-the-symbol as an overindul-
gence in literature, then it will be desirable to continue an inspection of the building's exterior. It is not an easy decision to make. For the vertical surface of the
church wall slices both the higher and lower approach roads like a knife; and,
when this psychological obstacle is penetrated, though something of the interior
workings of the convent is at last presented, a further discovery is made. The visitor now finds that the anticipated frontal views never do, in fact, materialize. He
becomes aware that the only surface of the building which actively encourages a
frontal inspection is indeed exactly that north wall of the church which he had
supposed was never to be interpreted in this way.

Thus, while other exposures, east and west, at the price of uncomfortable clam-
bering around, may certainly be seen in frontal alignment, they are usually presented, and apparently intended to be seen, only in a rapid foreshortening. Thus,
the south elevation, although generally visible in far less abrupt perspective, is still
evidently to be seen from oblique points of view (Plate 73); and thus, though on
three sides the monastery of La Tourette is entirely open to the landscape, the
conditions of its visibility lead, not to the seeing of the real and tangible voids,
but to a consciousness of solids (Plate 74), to an awareness of ranges of verticals
implicated in quick succession, of the returns of balconies rather than the presence of the windows at their rear. While, in addition, since externally the building
has an extremely high visual center of gravity, it must also be noticed that the
same solidity, the same optical closure which issues from the lateral foreshorten-
ings, is further affirmed by the vertical movements of the eye. Here again, as the
eye moves up and down, there is a distinct tendency for it to register the density
of undersurfaces and to infer the closest interrelation of horizontal memberings.

Once more, this elaborate divorce of physical reality and optical impression may
possibly be uncontrived; but, to the degree in which it sustains images of concentration and inwardness, and in the manner by which it makes prominent the behavior of the approach facade, it is a phenomenon which may at least *begin* to
suggest that we are in the presence of the most self-conscious resolution. On the
Acropolis, the Greeks, we are told, "employed the most learned deformations,
applying to their contours an impeccable adjustment to the laws of optics";[3] and,
though we are by no means on the Acropolis, if at this stage the patience can be
summoned to reexamine the north wall of the church, there may now be detected
admonitory signs which seem to rehearse the types of experience to which one is
later subjected.

First, just as at La Chaux-de-Fonds, where the blank panel generates a fluctuation of meaning and value and is incessantly transposed from a positive to a nega-

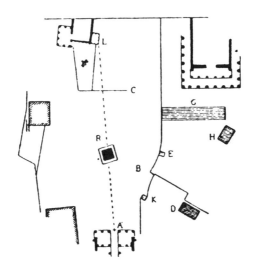

## THE ACROPOLIS, ATHENS

Figure 22   Acropolis, Athens, From Le
Corbusier, *Towards a New Architecture*.

tive role in the facade, so at La Tourette: the wall of the church, which is constantly invested with high figurative content and then deprived of it, acts both to
call attention to itself and simultaneously to shift attention outward onto the
visual field of which it is the principal component. But, while at La Chaux-de-
Fonds the fundamental structure of the ambiguity is simple, while this structure is
confined to a plane and causes largely an oscillation in the evaluation of surface,
at La Tourette we are presented with a far more evasive condition. It is a condition which involves above all readings of depth; and, while from it there issues a
series of disturbances scarcely amenable to any accurate generalization, there are
still two approximate tendencies which might be noticed: that the building tends
to revolve, to pivot around an imaginary central spike, and, at the same time, that
the building also tends to a supremely static behavior.

As has been inferred, Le Corbusier presents the north side of his church to the
visitor in very much the same way that in *Towards a New Architecture* he chose
to illustrate the Parthenon (Figure 22). He provides, that is, a type of foreshort-
ened frontal perspective which gives importance to the receding orthogonals, but
which firmly insists on the priority of the transversals. He offers, in other words, a
modified three-quarter view rather than a definitely oblique condition; and the
visitor is thus made aware of the monastery's western exposure as a significant,
but as a nevertheless subordinate, component of the principal figure.

But not to labor this point: at the same time that he does this, it is remarkable
that Le Corbusier has also built into this frontal plane a depth which by no means
exists in reality. The oblique cut of his parapet should now be noticed. It is a line
so slightly out of the horizontal that the eye has an instinctive tendency to 'correct' and translate it for what average experience suggests that it should be. For,
being eager to see it as the normal termination of a vertical plane, the eye is consequently willing to read it, not as the diagonal which physically it happens to be,
but as the element in a perspective recession which psychologically it seems. Le
Corbusier has established a 'false right angle';[4] and this *fausse équerre*, which in
itself infers depth, may also be seen as sporadically collaborating with the slope of
the ground further to sponsor an intermittent illusion that the building is revolv-
ing.

Something of the vital animation of surface, the small but sudden tremor of
mobility, in the area between bastion and belfry certainly derives from the torsion
to which the wall is thus subjected; but, if this phenomenal warping of surface
may be distinctly assisted by the real flexions of the bastion wall itself, then at

this point it should also be observed how the three *canons à lumière* now introduce a counteractive stress.

For the spectacle of the building as seen on arrival is finally predicated on a basis, not of one spiral, but of two. On the one hand there are the pseudoorthogonals which, by the complement they provide to the genuine recession of the monastery's west facade, serve to stimulate an illusion of rotation and spinning. But, on the other, are those three, twisting, writhing, and even agonized light sources—they illuminate the Chapel of the Holy Sacrament—which cause a quite independent and equally powerful moment of convolution. A pictorial opportunism lies behind the one tendency. A sculptural opportunism lies behind the other. There is a spiral in two dimensions. There is a contradictory spiral in three. A corkscrew is in competition with a restlessly deflective plane. Their equivocal interplay makes the building. And, since the coiled, columnar vortex, implied by the space rising above the chapel, is a volume which, like all vortices, has the cyclonic power to suck less energetic material in towards its axis of excitement, so the three *canons à lumière* conspire with the elements guaranteeing hallucination to act as a kind of tether securing a tensile equilibrium.

Now it is of the nature of optical illusions not to be apparent. They would have no value if they were. To operate, their behavior must be insidious; and to be justified, they must, probably, be something over and above 'mere' exercises in virtuosity. An estimate of the critical problem which they present—how surface becomes a revelation of depth, how depth becomes the instrument through which surface is represented, how a feeling of almost Romanesque density may be induced by a largely perforated construct—can scarcely be reached without some theory of the role which dissimulation must necessarily play in all perceptual structures; and such a theory can scarcely be presented here. Indeed so much time has here only been devoted to this matter—to this frontispiece which is also a profile, to these voids which act as solids, to this manifold intercourse between the static and the mobile—because, in certain ways, these manifestations seem to constitute an important datum which, if we fail to interpret it, may hopelessly distort any analysis of the building which lies behind these externals.

"The struggle goes on inside hidden on the surface" says Le Corbusier in another context;[5] and if, for the moment, enough may have been said to suggest the perceptual intricacies of La Tourette even before the building has been entered, it must now be possible to approach it with entirely opposite and wholly conceptual criteria in mind. Thus, though the normal way of seeing a building is as here described—from the outside in, since the normal way of conceiving one is supposed to be from the inside out, it may now be convenient to withdraw attention from the more sensational aspects of the monastery and to consider instead its ostensible rationale.

The program for the building was explicit. There was to be a church to which the public could, on occasion, be admitted. There were to be one hundred cells for professors and students, an oratory, a dining room, a library, classrooms, and spaces for conference and recreation. There was a certain problem of institutional decorum. But, though the architect was therefore subjected to certain very definite limitations, and though he was involved with a religious order whose regime was established rather more than seven centuries ago, it cannot truthfully be claimed that the operational requirements with which he was confronted were so very rigid and inflexible as to predicate any inevitable solution.

It is possible to imagine the Wrightian version of this program: a major hexagonoid volume, proliferating by an inward impulse a variety of minor hexagonoids, terraces, and covered ways. A Miesian solution can be conceived. Embryos of the Aaltoesque, the Kahnian and a whole forest of other variants swarm in the imagination. But the number of choices available to any one man, like those available to any one epoch, are never as great as those which, in fact, exist. Like the epoch, the man has his *style*—the sum total of the emotional dispositions, the mental biases, and the characteristic acts which, taken together, comprise his existence; and, in its essential distributions (though with one great exception), Le Corbusier's building is coordinated very much along the lines that previous evidence of his style might have led one to predict.

The solution which he has presented—a quadrilateral pierced by a courtyard; with the church on its north side; with the cells deployed to east, south, and west in two tiers immediately below the roof; with the library, classrooms, oratory, and principal entrance on the floor below this; with the refectory, chapter house, and major circulations at the still lower level adjacent to the floor of the church— is entirely evident from the published plans of the building; and, like all Le Corbusier's solutions, it is both a highly generalized as well as a highly particularized statement.

It could be said that La Tourette, like any other building by any other architect, is primarily determined by a formal statement which is felt to be a logical one. Obviously it reflects Le Corbusier's insistence on volumetric economy; and it would be reasonable, therefore, to suggest that the final premises of the arguments on which it is based are not really susceptible to empirical proof. Secondarily, the monastery would seem to be determined on the basis of category, i.e., by its relation to a series of propositions which postulate the ideal form of the Dominican establishment, conceived in the abstract, and presumed to be valid irrespective of the circumstances of place or time. And, finally, these more or less aprioristic deductions are brought into antithetical connection with specific conditions of locality.

The site was allegedly of Le Corbusier's own choosing. It could be supposed that other architects might have chosen otherwise. But, if a superb prospect verified the selection, it does also seem probable that this particular terrain was chosen for its inherent difficulties. For at La Tourette the site is both everything and nothing. It is equipped with an abrupt slope and a lavishly accidental cross fall. It is by no means the local condition which would readily justify that quintessential Dominican establishment which seems to have been preconceived. Rather it is the reverse: and architecture and landscape, lucid and separate experiences, are like the rival protagonists of a debate who progressively contradict and clarify each other's meaning.

Above all, the nature of their interaction is dialectical; and thus the building, with its church to the north, liturgically correct in orientation, separated from but adjoining the living quarters which face the sun, is presented as though it were a thesis for discussion; and thus the site inevitably rises to function as counterproposition. There is a statement of presumed universals and a contrary statement of particulars. There is the realist proclamation and the nominalist response, the idealist gesture, the empiricist veto. But if this is a procedure with which Le Corbusier has long since made us familiar, and if such is his particular mode of logic, there is, of course, here in the program a curiously pragmatic justification for its exercise. For it was, after all, a Dominican monastery which was here required. An architectural dialectician, the greatest, was to service the requirements of the archsophisticates of dialectic; and there was, therefore, a quite specially appropriate dimension which inhered to the approach.

But, if the building thus answers to the ethos of the institution, this was surely the mere accident of parallel attitudes, of equivalent rigor. The architect scarcely set out deliberately to provide the plastic analogue of scholastic debate. It was only that his state of mind and that of his clients were coincident in their astringent quality, and that both parties were ironically aware of their common identity and difference. Above all, it was not a case of the architect mimicking scholastic reasoning so much as it was the presence, on both sides, of irreproachable intellectual integrity which has disinfected the logical conclusions of the argument of all those conciliatory flavorings which are apt to be the outcome of attempts to bring religious institutions and modern architecture into accord. At La Tourette there are no turgid atmospherics. There is nothing ingratiating or cheap; and, as a result, the building becomes positive in its negation of compromise. It is not so much a church with living quarters attached as it is a domestic theater for virtuosi of asceticism with, adjoining it, a gymnasium for the exercise of spiritual athletes. The figure of the boxer and his punch bag on the terrace of the 1928 project for Geneva has become conflated with the image of Jacob wrestling with the Angel.

However, this is to discuss effects before causes. The play on spiritual exercise as physical gymnastic may be one of the more invigorating themes at La Tourette; but it is a result rather than a determinant, and the immediate causation of the building, apart from the dialectic of architecture and site, ought now at least briefly to be noticed. While, since Le Corbusier has always been frugal with ideas and has never mistaken mere experiment or intellectual profligacy for thoughtfulness, the more obvious causation is not far to seek.

There is the famous structural scheme for the Maison Domino (Plate 12), with its conception of space as something horizontally stratified like the layers of a Neapolitan wafer; and there are the corollaries to this drawing: A denial of the spatial expression of the structural cell, a relegation of the column to the status of punctuation or *caesura*, and a penetration of the resultant product by a labyrinthine construction of miscellaneous partitions which propagate a centrifugal stress. This seems to be almost all. Basically, it is all by now very old; and, as a result, there appears to be very little to say about the living quarters of the monastery taken by themselves.

There are the usual elements of wit: an entrance which is possibly a little too Japanese, and the five parlors adjoining it; a spiral staircase which parodies something from a mediaeval building; and the astonishing Ledolcian fantasy of the oratory as seen from outside (Plate 74). But these are the *quodlibets* of the scholastic discourse; and more important are the distinctions of emotional tone which the different levels of the living quarters support. These are affected by an orchestration of light. There is a movement from the brilliance and lateral extension of the refectory and chapter house, through the more somber tonality of the library and the oratory, up to the relative darkness and lateral closure of the cells. There are the progressive degrees of concentration and intimacy; but if, in their turn, the cells—each equipped with its own blank white panel—are like a hundred private recapitulations of the church, it is now necessary to close the circuit and to approach this most problematic element.

And, in this context, let us first notice Le Corbusier's passion for walls:

The elements of the site rise up like walls, panoplied in the power of their cubic co-efficient, stratification, material, etc.; like the walls of a room.

Our elements are vertical walls.

The ancients built walls, walls which stretch out to meet and amplify the wall.

There are no other architectural elements internally: light and its reflection in a great flood by the walls and the floor, which is really a horizontal wall.[6]

The inordinate significance which the vertical plane has always possessed for Le Corbusier has been somewhat obscured by his own polemic, so that we are apt to think that the logical development of the Maison Domino structure is no more than its packaging in a suitable cellophane envelope. And, in such an envelope, the conceptual reality of this scheme is, of course, entirely clear. There are pancakes supported on pins. It is all visible; and it is all somewhat like the diagrams which recur again and again as we turn over the pages of *Précisions* or the earlier volumes of the *Oeuvre complète.*

But, although brilliant and cogent analysis of conceptual reality has always been one aspect of Le Corbusier's achievement, he has rarely, in his constructed works, paraded analysis as solution. He is one of the few architects who have suppressed the demands of neither sensation nor thought. Between thought and sensation he has always maintained a balance; and therefore—and almost with him alone—while the intellect civilizes the sensible, the sensible actualizes civility. This is the obvious message; and thus, with Le Corbusier, the conceptual argument never really provides a sufficient pretext but has always to be reinterpreted in terms of perceptual compulsions.

Hence, at La Tourette, all elements can be referred to two distinct structures of argument. The inclination of the parapet of the church *may* be related to optical desiderata; but it may also, *and just as well*, be related to the necessity of articulating a functionally distinct volume as something to be identified as separate from the other three sides of a courtyard. Hence also, even though the plan may be "the determination of everything . . . an austere abstraction, an algebrization and cold of aspect,"[7] the generational prime cause of Le Corbusier's buildings may be just as much a matter of their vertical as of their horizontal planes.

"The floor which is really a horizontal wall": an assertion of this order would have offended the structural sense of Frank Lloyd Wright. Nor would the inference that floors and walls are interchangeable planes, capable of identical determination, be any more acceptable to a Miesian rationalist. But, though it is not so much a definition as a casual aside, this sort of pronouncement could very possibly be pressed into service partly to explain the church, the most audacious innovation which La Tourette presents. For, if floors are horizontal walls, then, presumably, walls are vertical floors; and, while elevations become plans and the building a form of dice, then the complete aplomb with which Le Corbusier manages his church may, in some faint degree, be explained.

The quality of the church, in which chiaroscural effects reach their maximum, in which negation becomes positive, is not to be photographed. But, perhaps as a form, it is to be related, not as at first may appear to a late Gothic prototype—some King's College Chapel or Franciscan structure in the Valley of Mexico—but to Le Corbusier's own (and contemporaneous) Boîte à Miracles from the Tokyo Museum (Figure 23). This 'Box of Miracles,' intended as the stage of an open-air theater, although it scarcely displays the same attenuated volume, does show the same slightly oblique cut in its roof, a similar entrance condition from the side, and an identical hangarlike appearance. To borrow a term from Vincent Scully, it is one of Le Corbusier's *megaron volumes,*[8] one of those tunnel spaces compressed between vertical planes which, deriving from the *Maison Citrohan* (Figure 24), have persisted in his work alongside those more advertised *sandwich volumes* where the pressure of the horizontal planes is the more acute.

A history of the crossfertilization of the megaron and sandwich concepts throughout Le Corbusier's career would be entirely relevant to the discussion of La Tourette; but it is scarcely an account which can fall within the scope of a short critique. Here one can only distinguish that Poissy is a sandwich and that the Maison Citrohan is the basic megaron, that the sandwich concept emphasizes floors and the megaron concept walls. But though, like all oversimple classifications, this one, if pressed, could easily become facetious, what is remarkable about it is that such a differentiation of species is less easily made than at first seems likely. For we are faced, yet again, with a house like Garches and we ask what it is. Is it a sandwich? Or is it a megaron? Do we feel the pressure of the floors or do we feel the pressure of the end walls?

The hybrid condition of Garches perhaps establishes some rather crude platform from which to view the intervening years. A megaron which is anxious to become a sandwich (or vice versa), it partly illustrates a line of development leading through to Poissy and to the Le Corbusier of the early thirties. But, at Garches, there are also those two frontispieces, the entrance and the garden elevations, which are scarcely connected with either the sandwich or the megaron idea. In terms of the lateral walls of the house they do not logically exploit the theme of an open-ended box. In terms of the floors, these facades conceal rather than expose the reality of the structural components. They are articulated—by a series of

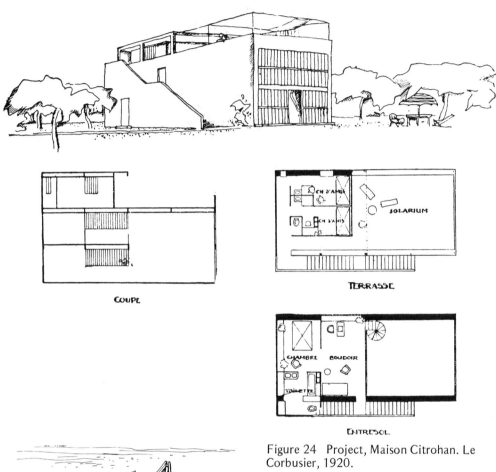

COUPE

TERRASSE

CH D'AMIS

CH D'AMIS

SOLARIUM

CHAMBRE     BOUDOIR

TOILETTE

ENTRESOL

Figure 24   Project, Maison Citrohan. Le Corbusier, 1920.

Figure 23   Project, Tokyo Museum, Tokyo. Box of Miracles. Le Corbusier, 1956 (?).

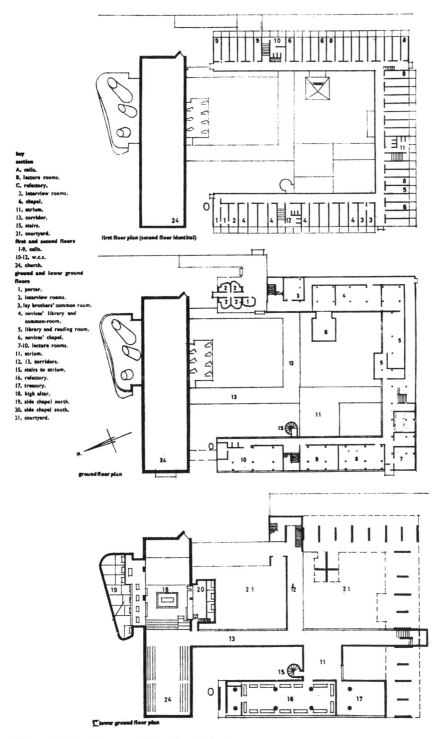

key
section
A, cells.
B, lecture rooms.
C, refectory.
  2, interview rooms.
  6, chapel.
11, atrium.
13, corridor.
15, stairs.
21, courtyard.
first and second floors
  1-9, cells.
10-12, w.c.s.
24, church.
ground and lower ground
floors
  1, porter.
  2, interview rooms.
  3, lay brothers' common room.
  4, novices' library and
    common-room.
  5, library and reading room.
  6, novices' chapel.
  7-10, lecture rooms.
11, atrium.
12, 13, corridors.
15, stairs to atrium.
16, refectory.
17, treasury.
18, high altar.
19, side chapel north.
20, side chapel south.
21, courtyard.

first floor plan (second floor identical)

ground floor plan

lower ground floor plan

Figure 25    La Tourette. Plans. Le Corbusier.

horizontal dissections and antigravitational cuts—so as to *comply* with a structural argument; but, in terms of an entirely literal induction from the physique of the building, they can only be considered a *non sequitur.*

Like so many other Corbusian elements they are obedient to the exigencies of the eye rather than those of the work, to the needs of the conceiving subject rather than the perceived object. They are the stimulants of heightened sensation. Their predicament is optical. Their logical reason for existence is stereographic. They delineate. They are the superficies by which the eye measures the specific gravity of the block behind, the two-dimensional surfaces on which the density of a three-dimensional substance is registered and inscribed, they are the planes which volatilize the reading of depth.

But this is to parenthesize. For, though the ability to charge depth with surface, to condense spatial concavities into plane, to drag to its most eloquent pitch the dichotomy between the rotund and the flat is the absolutely distinguishing mark of Le Corbusier's later style, the cerebrality which typifies Garches is not prominent at La Tourette. In spite of its dialectic, the Dominican convent is far from an intellectualistic building; but if, like Garches, it presents itself as a single block, then, unlike Garches, it is a block which, if examined in terms of plan, appears at first to contain in the church a major violation of all logical consistency (Figure 25).

To a block one attributes a structural continuity, a textural consistency of space, and a homogeneity of spatial grain or layering. While recognizing it to be hollow and to be empty, one still conceives of its emptiness as, in some way, the metaphor for a block of stone or a block of wood. It is exploitable only on the condition of collaborating with the nature which it has been assumed to possess.

Or so it might have been thought. But, at La Tourette, these precepts—which one may believe Le Corbusier himself to have taught and which one may feel to be a norm of procedure—are conspicuously breached, and breached with a sophistication so covert as to provide a new area of experience. By cramming a Tokyo-type megaron, the church, and a Poissy-type sandwich, the living quarters, into the closest proximity, by jamming two discrete elements into the same volume, from the violation of a unity of conception, it has become possible, simultaneously, to manipulate all spatial coefficients. In other words, by a combination of themes that one might have thought were obliged to remain forever separate, Le Corbusier has been able to instigate sensations of both tension and compression, openness and density, torsion and stability; and, by doing so, he has been able to guarantee a visual stimulus so acute that only very retrospectively does the observer begin to be aware of the abnormal experience to which he has been subjected.

Notes

1 José Ortega y Gasset, *Meditations on Quixote*, New York, 1961, pp. 68-69. This book first appeared in Madrid in 1914.

2 Le Corbusier, *Vers une architecture*, Paris, ed. 1958, pp. 39, 154, 166.

3 *Ibid.*, p. 170.

4 *Ibid.*, p. 39.

5 Le Corbusier, *Creation is a Patient Search*, New York, 1960, p. 219.

6 Le Corbusier, *Vers une architecture*, pp. 149-50.

7 Le Corbusier, *ibid.*, p. 145. This statement is a quotation given without source. (Does it derive from Guadet?)

8 Vincent Scully, *Modern Architecture*, New York, 1961, p. 42.

Plate 70   La Tourette. Aerial view from the north. Le Corbusier, 1956-57.

Plate 71   La Tourette. North wall of church.

Plate 72   La Tourette. View from the north-west.

Plate 73   La Tourette. View from the south-
east.

Plate 74   La Tourette. Detail of east elevation.

# The Architecture of Utopia

First published in *Granta*, 1959.

For unto you is paradise opened, the tree of life is planted, the time to come is prepared, plenteousness is made ready, a city is builded, and rest is allowed, yea perfect goodness and wisdom. The root of evil is sealed up from you, weakness and the moth is hid from you, and corruption is fled into hell to be forgotten. Sorrows are passed, and in the end is shewed the treasure of immortality.

—2 Esdras 8: 52-54

Utopia and the image of a city are inseparable. And if, as we might suppose, Utopia does find one of its roots in Jewish millennial thought, the reason is not far to seek. "A city is builded and is set upon a broad field and is full of good things." "Glorious things are spoken of thee, O city of God." "And he carried me away in the spirit to a great and high mountain, and showed me that great city, the holy Jerusalem, descending out of heaven from God." Such biblical references to the felicity of a promised city are too abundant to ignore; but, for all that, the ingredients of the later *Civitas Dei* are as much Platonic as Hebraic and certainly it is a distinctly Platonic deity which presides over the first Utopias to assume specific and architectural form.

Architecture serves practical ends, it is subjected to use; but it is also shaped by ideas and fantasies, and these it can classify, crystallize, and make visible. Very occasionally indeed the architectural crystallization of an idea may even precede the literary one; and thus, if we can consider the Renaissance concept of the ideal city to be Utopian—as surely we may—we find here a notable case of architectural priority. For Thomas More's famous book did not appear until 1516; and by this time the Utopian theme had been well established—in Italian architecture, at least—for almost half a century. Filarete's Sforzinda, the paradigmatic city of so many future Utopian essays, had been projected *c.* 1460; and although Scamozzi's Palma Nova, the first ideal city to achieve concrete form, was not realized until 1593, the themes which it employs were a common architectural currency by 1500.

As illustrated by Sforzinda and Palma Nova (Plates 75 and 76), the ideal city is usually circular; and, as More said of the towns of his own Utopia, "He that knows one knows them all, they are so alike one another, except where the situation makes some difference."[1] One may withdraw in horror from this calculated elimination of variety; and quite rightly so, for the ideal city, though an entertaining type to inspect, is often a somewhat monotonous environment. But then the ideal city, like Utopia itself, should scarcely be judged in these immediate physical terms. Nor should we evaluate it by either visual or practical criteria, for its rationale is cosmic and metaphysical; and here, of course, lies its peculiar ability to impose itself on the mind.

An architect of the Renaissance, had he felt it necessary to argue about circular, centralized, and radial exercises such as *Palma Nova*, to justify them might possibly have quoted the account in the *Timaeus* where the Demiurge is described as fashioning the universe "in a spherical shape, in which all the radii from the middle are equally distant from the bounding extremities; as this is the most perfect of all figures and the most similar to himself."[2] And thus, the Renaissance architect might have concluded, as an analogy of this divinely created sphere and as an emblem of the artificer who is declared to be immanent within it, the city receives its circular outline.

Now it is by association with the emblematic significance of the sphere that we can understand the persistence of the circular form throughout by far the greater number of architectural Utopias; and so long as our mental inflection is Platonic, as a setting for the headquarters of an ideal state the ideal form of the circle, the mirror of a harmonious cosmic order, follows quite naturally. Thus, on through the seventeenth, eighteenth, and even nineteenth centuries—even as late as 1898 in Ebenezer Howard's prototype for Letchworth Garden City—we still find the circle or conspicuous traces of it.

But there is perhaps another argument involved in this choice of form which is not only Platonic in its bias but also Christian. For possibly the circle is intended both to signify and to assist a redemption of society. It is said to be a natural shape. As obviously, if it is the shape of the universe, it must be. "It is manifest that nature delights principally in round figures, since we find that most things which are generated, made or directed by nature are round."[3] The dictum is from Alberti, one of the first architects to bring a typically Renaissance intellect to bear upon the problems of the city; but the opinion is by no means peculiar to him. Rather, it reflects the characteristic tone of quattrocento humanism; and the argument that the circular city is predominantly 'natural' (not at all incongruous with the argument that it is divine), must evidently have introduced a powerful predisposition in its favor. For if a circular city might now be considered to exemplify the laws of nature, how unnatural and therefore in a sense how 'fallen' the medieval city must have seemed; while if the medieval city could be thus seen as a counterpart to Babylon, almost as illustration of the working of original sin, the humanistic version of the New Jerusalem could now very well be experienced as the symbol of a regenerated humanity, or a restoration of the injuries of time.

Thus, if nature takes pleasure in the circle (and gives second preference to the square), it is to be expected that these forms should recur elsewhere within the fabric of a Utopian town; and Campanella, for instance, describes, in his *Città del*

*Sole*, a church that is placed in the center of the town and which "is perfectly round, free on all sides, but supported by massive and elegant columns," a church in which "on the altar is nothing but two globes, of which the larger is a celestial, the smaller a terrestrial one, and in the dome are painted the stars of the sky." But, again, the church which is thus specified had been long anticipated by architects. "We cannot doubt that the little temples we make ought to resemble this very great one, which by His immense goodness was perfectly completed with one word of His."[4] This is the opinion of Palladio, and it was also his practice; but Campanella's church and Palladio's advice are already previsioned by the central building in the *Perspective of a Square* (Plate 77), variously attributed to Luciano Laurana, Francesco Di Giorgio, or Piero della Francesca and executed *c.* 1470.

Here it might be said that we are shown Utopia infiltrating a preexisting reality; but, nevertheless, this picture can quite well be allowed to serve as a representation of just the city which humanist thought envisaged. "The place where you intend to fix a temple," Alberti recommends, "ought to be noted, famous, and indeed stately, clear from all contagion of secular things";[5] and, following his advice, not only is this particular church round, but the square in which it stands is mathematically proportioned according to Pythagorean principles, while the little palaces about it, grave, regular, and serene, complete the illusion that we have indeed entered into a world where perfect equilibrium is the law.

Fully to understand the revolutionary quality of this space, one should compare it with some medieval square (which, incidentally, one might prefer); and one should compare it then with its innumerable and rather belated progeny. No space of quite this order and regularity came into existence until Michelangelo began his Campidoglio *c.* 1546, and scarcely any space of comparable order was attempted until the seventeenth century. In Paris the Place des Vosges was conceived in 1603. In London the Piazza of Covent Garden dates from the 1630s.

And the same may be said of the *Street Scene* attributed to Bramante (Plate 78), which provides an urbanistic motif first to be realized in the theater before achieving a more permanent form in building. For it was not until the pontificate of Sixtus V, determined as he was to transform Rome into a modern city, that this kind of straight, serious, and majestic thoroughfare became something which no great city was to be considered complete without. While it is surely equivalent streets which Wren proposed for London, it is again some diluted Napoleonic memory of this avenue of palaces and its closing triumphal arch which persists in the Champs Elysées and in all those innumerable boulevards in Paris and elsewhere that arose to imitate it.

However, the success of the small circular church—which Alberti, in humanist style, insisted on calling a temple—was even greater. Already built by 1502, the dimunitive Tempietto of San Pietro in Montorio summarized themes which were then to be monumentally exploited in Michelangelo's St. Peter's, were to be taken up in France, to recur in St. Paul's, to become Hawksmoor's magnificent mausoleum at Castle Howard, and which in Oxford, again set down in the middle of a square, still present themselves for our inspection as the Radcliffe Library.

But we must beware of overstatement; and quite simply to propose all these spaces, all these squares and buildings to be Utopian is to be guilty of obvious overstatement. The Radcliffe Camera, for instance, or the Place des Vosges can scarcely be called Utopian without considerable qualification of this term. For we can scarcely suppose that their respective sponsors, either Oxford or Henri IV, would seriously have been disposed to spend large amounts of capital simply in order to exhibit the plastic corollary to highly abstract political speculation. So much is clear; and yet the Radcliffe Camera and the Place des Vosges, neither of them exactly revolutionary manifestations, are both of them still the products of an architectural culture which had long accepted the once revolutionary *città ideale* as axiomatic and which habitually derived all the conventional elements of its repertory from this city's accessories. May we not then propose, by way of qualification, that these architectural manifestations, though not in the strict sense Utopian, are still a complement to Utopian thought? That they rose to satisfy emotional needs awakened by humanistic speculation? And that they are products of the same impulse which made of the New Jerusalem an instrument for reshaping the world?

So much may be proposed; but there is still an element of irony which attaches itself to any realization of the Utopian vision. Transcending reality as it does, transforming it as it may, Utopia becomes increasingly compromised as it becomes increasingly acceptable. Notoriously, the configuration of the ideal city was 'ideal' not only for the philosopher but also for the military engineer; and while the first of such cities, Palma Nova, was established as a Venetian military station towards the Istrian frontier, others, very many with names famous in the history of war, were 'idealized' rather through an application to the laws of ballistics than through any devotion to the principles of Plato.[7]

In these and other ways we might demonstrate how a revolutionary idea transforms not only the world but also itself. Penetrating that establishment which it seeks to subvert, permeating it, providing its own color and tone, Utopia ultimately becomes the *ancien régime* against which new demonstrations arise. But the constellation of ideas, partly Christian, partly Platonic, in some senses scientific, which presided over the inception of the late fifteenth century vision could scarcely be expected to occur again, and no subsequent Utopia has ever been able to command an architectural enthusiasm so concentrated and intense as that which Renaissance humanism could draw upon. Thus the successors of the humanists, the philosophers of the Enlightenment, conscious though they might have been of imperfections in the world which they occupied, were only rarely able to enlist the services of their architectural contemporaries.

For these reasons, in the project by Ledoux of 1776 (Plate 79)—which we might envisage as typifying the Utopian conditions that the Enlightenment conceived— the circular form seems largely to survive as an intelligible convention. It cannot be wholly sacrificed. Nor can it be wholly convincing. For though the rather deistic turn of mind exhibited by Ledoux might very well be able to accept a circular disposition for cities, for churches, and even for strange cemetery-catacombs— even though a Boullée could find it the supremely appropriate configuration for the Cenotaph for Newton (Plate 80)—the concept is no longer quite so 'natural' as it once had been; and though a Renaissance idea of 'nature' might still provide the mold for revolutionary form, it could no longer wholly absorb the sympathies of that new kind of 'natural' man which the impending revolution itself was to evoke.

Romantic individualism and the concept of Utopia were scarcely to be fused; and, as a result, in the nineteenth century the Utopian idea was able to draw on no first-class architectural talent. It persisted, and even proliferated; but it persisted as regards architecture chiefly as a subterranean tradition. Neither the average nor the exceptional nineteenth century architect were ever to be much seduced by Benthamite principles of utility or Positivistic schemes of social reform; so that, in default of the architect's interest, the nineteenth century Utopia retains much of the stamp which the Italians had put upon it between three and four hundred years ago.

But it had in any case become a somewhat provincial idea;[8] and to the better minds of the time, often heavily influenced by subtle hypotheses as to the 'organic' nature of society, the *appearance* of Utopia must have come to seem unduly mechanical.[9] Accordingly, deserted by intellect, Utopia now becomes naive; and while its Platonic forms persist they are no longer infused with a corresponding content. Also, Utopia seems now to have descended the social scale; for it is apparently no longer concerned with the redemption of society as a whole, but only with the redemption of its lower strata. Therefore the nineteenth century Utopia is apt to wear a look of either strenuous philanthropy or equally strenuous self-help; and the *Happy Colony* "to be built by the working men of Britain in New Zealand" (Plate 81) might be taken as an example of the latter look. It is a delightful mid-Victorian proposition; but although in this engaging scheme so many of the former elements of Utopia survive—Platonic solids, delineations of the globe, and even a little central building which has ceased to function as a temple and become instead a model farm—still it is rather to be doubted whether such symbolism any longer had public significance or whether many of those to whom this project was addressed were conscious of its author's transpositions of the traditional iconography.

But, if one kind of Utopia has here received its ultimate formal degradation, can it be said that Utopia has been revived in our own day?

That there is, or rather was, a profound Utopian impulse in modern architecture is indisputable; and, much as one imagines the drawing boards of Renaissance Italy, the drawing boards of the earlier decades of this century certainly seem to have been cluttered with the abstracted images of cities. Two in particular deserve attention: the mechanistic, vitalistic city of the Futurists where dynamism was ceaseless and a life was promised approximating to an absolute orgy of flux (Plate 82); and another city which, though a metropolis, was curiously static and which seems to have been almost as empty of people as the square in the picture at Urbino. Something of the Futurist city has been a component of all subsequent development. But the success of the second city, Le Corbusier's ville radieuse (Plate 83) has been inordinate; so that, for the present, one could safely assert that this is the image of the city which controls. Never perhaps to be realized as a whole, its accessories, like those of Sforzinda, have everywhere been adopted. But, if in reality the ville radieuse would be almost as boring as Sforzinda before it, if it has a similar schematic monotony, if, like Sforzinda, it is perhaps one of those general ideas which can never be erased, one of those high abstractions which are empowered to perpetuate themselves, does this make of it a Utopia in the sense which we have so considered Sforzinda?

If Utopias are what Karl Mannheim defines them to be: "orientations transcending reality . . . which, when they pass over into conduct, tend to shatter, either partially or wholly, the order of things prevailing at the time,"[10]  then we must surely concede that the ville radieuse is an instrument of some power. But, if we ask with what ideas an 'orientation' which 'transcends reality' is constructed we are obliged to wonder whether contemporary society can really tolerate such an 'orientation.'

Judged in terms of results, the most viable Utopia was certainly that evolved *c.* 1500 and which, to borrow a phrase from Jacob Burckhardt, might conveniently be described as an attempt to turn the state into a work of art. Now need we say that the state never can be turned into a work of art? That the attempt to do so is the attempt to bring time to a stop, the impossible attempt to arrest growth and motion? For the work of art (which is also an attempt to bring time to a stop), once it has left its maker, is not subject to change. It enjoys neither growth nor motion. Its mode of existence is not biological. And, though it may instruct, civilize, and even edify the individual who is exposed to it, in itself the work of art will remain constant. For the work of art is not life; and nor, for that matter, is Utopia politics. But in the relation of the individual with the work of art we may still see something comparable to the relation of the state with Utopia. For Utopia too may instruct, civilize, and even edify the political society which is exposed to it. It may do all this; but for all that it cannot, any more than the work of art, become alive. It cannot, that is, *become* the society which it changes; and it cannot therefore change itself.

A crude naturalism experiences great difficulty in recognizing these existential conditions of the Utopian idea; and, to continue the analogy, a crude naturalism approaches Utopia very much indeed as the vulgar are supposed to approach a work of art. It demands an immediate effect. The work of art is *like* life. Utopia is *like* politics. Then let them be so. But the demand that Utopia approximate to a portrait at the Royal Academy or a novel by Arnold Bennett is conceivably more innocent than vulgar. For while the mimetic intention of both art and Utopia requires no emphasis, neither can properly 'imitate' life or society except after their own laws—laws which, to all appearance, four hundred and fifty years ago were wonderfully identical. Indeed, at a much later date, Sir Joshua Reynolds' outrageous pronouncement that "the whole beauty and grandeur of art consists in being able to get above all singular forms, local customs, particularities, and de-tails of every kind,"[11] might very well be a definition of "the whole beauty and grandeur" of Utopia. But it is also a statement of classical artistic doctrine, and it introduces the problem of whether we are able to detach Utopia from classicism.

Perhaps with difficulty we may: but only surely if we are prepared to recognize Utopia's limitations; and only too if, while recognizing them, we are also prepared to remember that Utopia is defined as an 'orientation' which 'transcends reality.' Then, and armed with this definition, we might even conclude that, when 'reality' is primarily attributed to motion, growth, change, and history, then the preemi-nent 'reality-transcending orientation,' the obvious Utopia, might evidently be something not too far removed from that persistent image which has so often been the instrument of change—the classical image of changelessness.

Addendum 1973

And the classical image of changelessness, that impossible image which has yet been responsible for more changes than one would wish to think about, is so important to this discussion that it might be useful to introduce a rather more strict definition of Utopia than Karl Mannheim's.

**A Utopian conception in its fully developed form might be defined as a unified vision which includes:**

1. a carefully considered artistic theory or attitude towards art integrated with
2. a fully developed political and social structure conceived of as extant in
3. a locus independent of time, place, history or accident.[12]

Now, for obvious reasons, no Utopian speculator—be he philosopher, architect, or absolute despot—was ever able to combine all these themes. But, if we are here in the realm of myth and if to combine all these themes was a patent impossibility for the speculative intellect of the Renaissance and the Enlightenment (which had a high regard for them all), any comparable endeavor is surely an even more patent impossibility for us at the present day.

We may, indeed, hunger and thirst after righteousness and our moral zeal may well be effusive; but whether our moral passion will, or should, overcome our intellectual fastidiousness must be another matter. We may agonize over a supposed prevalent absence of Utopian reference; but, however much it may be often considered to be so, the relation of society to Utopia is not the relation of a donkey to a carrot. Utopia is an optimum and, therefore, an end condition. Such are the terms of its alliance with classicism. A particular Utopia can be subjected to neither alteration, addition, nor subtraction;[13] but, while recognizing this, if we go on to observe the constantly expressed preference of the present day for the dynamic rather than the static, for becoming rather than being, for process rather than product, perhaps for effort rather than achievement, we can only begin to define a situation which is inimical to the idea of Utopia. And if we then go on to observe our interest in the concrete and the specific, in the paradoxical, in things as found, if we notice our preference for toughness, difficulty, and complication, our insistence on the empirical fact, on data collection, our belief in the work of art as an issue of tensions and balances, as a reconciliation of discordances and opposites, as something essentially and absolutely located in time and place, as something which presents and re-presents its temporal and spatial limitations, as something growing from and thereby illustrating its liaison with existing society, as something intimately involved with particular technologies and with ascertainable functions and techniques, then this can only be still further to establish that the range of often contradictory ideas which we habitually entertain are, *if it is possible to take them together*, considerably more than distinctly hostile to any form of Utopian fantasy.

Or so one might have thought. But any such simple and tolerably commonsense conjecture can only be to deny the historical evidence that a mental orientation towards specifics and a proneness towards Utopian speculation, however logically incompatible they may be, have long been able to enjoy an apparently happy coexistence.

**I have a formal difficulty about the concept of Utopia ... Does the Utopian postulate a static Utopia, that is to say a society so perfect that any further change (improvement) is inconceivable? Or is Utopia dynamic, a state to which we are continually aspiring but never reach because it itself is continually changing, moving ahead of us? ... I cannot subscribe to the static version, for its assumptions are inherently absurd. . . .[14]**

So wrote one of the contributors to the issue of *Granta* in which this essay was first published; and his point of view is completely understandable—at least so long as we do not find Utopia to be a genuine problem or, alternatively, so long as we are willing directly to equate the notions of Utopia and social progress. However, if we approach Utopia with suspicion (Utopia where the citizens cannot fail to be happy because they cannot choose but be good), if we are sceptical of its combination of progressivism and classicism, then we might probably recognize that the imagined possible fusion of an evolutionary sequence with a perfected condition (of endless *becoming* which will, still, always be complete *being*) is one of the more extraordinary fantasies of the present day—a fantasy which is apt to seem always as wholly benign as it is undoubtedly, well intentioned.

The idea that society can approximate the condition of music, that change and order may become one and the same, that the roads leading into the future may now, for the first time, be rendered free of all bumps and impediments is, of course, one of the root fantasies of modern architecture; and it is apt to be one of those presumptions which travel unexamined. Utopia is both to bring time to an end and, simultaneously, it is to inaugurate an era in which the movements of time will be, for the most part, smooth and predictable. The notion of the millennium is to retain all of its old-style cosmic significance and is then to be made further agreeable by a redecoration with all the gloss of rationality and science.

The state of mind which is here implied, unembarrassed, superstitious, and allegedly enlightened, should now be recognized as constituting the major block to any contemporary Utopian formulation—should this be necessary. A state of mind well disposed toward what it supposes Utopia to be but unequipped with sense of metaphysical difficulty or reservation—the state of mind preeminently of the planner and the empirical sociologist—for the most part unaware of Utopia's historical origins and, generally, conceiving these to be irrelevant: what we have here is, very largely, the imposition of Hegel upon Plato and, further, the tacit insistence that the results of this condition are, necessarily, libertarian.

Which may be, rather extravagantly, to generalize and to jump; but which may also be, opportunistically, to identify those coercive attributes of Utopia which Karl Popper has selected to condemn. For Popper's criticisms of Utopia and the closed society,[15] though they were available to—and apparently ignored by—the contributors to *Granta*,[16] must be conceded as establishing a conspicuous obstacle both to the exercise of Utopian fantasy as well as to the deployment of most of the traditional programs/fantasies of modern architecture.

Utopia, because it implies a planned and hermetically sealed society, leads to suppression of diversity, intolerance, often to stasis presenting itself as change, and, ultimately, to violence. Or, more specifically: if Utopia proposes the achievement of abstract goods rather than the eradication of concrete evils then it is apt to be tyrannical: this since there can far more easily be consensus about concrete evils than there can be about abstract goods. Such is the Popperian message, which, supported as it is by a critique of determinism and a developed theory of the nature of investigation, remains hard to refute and which, very largely, continues to be ignored.

But, of course, when all this has been observed and taken to heart (which, in this context, might mean when modern architecture has been cut down to size and its intentions admitted to be poetry rather than prescription), the problem and the predicament of abstract goods in a world of concrete evils—always an acute question for the architect—remains unalleviated and unexamined; and, if one must agree with Popper about the obligation to eradicate concrete evils, then one must still notice that the issue of abstract goods (with all its Platonic, natural law, and modern-architecture overtones) emphatically persists. For how to designate specific evil without at least *some* theory of general good? And is not Popper's position yet another Utopian formulation—and a Utopian formulation which is particularly Germanic?

**The road to progress was not sought in external deeds or in revolutions, but exclusively in the inner constitution of man and its transformations.**

For again, Mannheim—with his discrimination of a largely apolitical and Germanic Utopia (*vide* note 8)—might seem to enter the picture, and Popper's ideal of emancipation through self-knowledge—an emancipation both for the individual and society (the Kantian ideal)—might seem to belong to this important, but still intrinsically local, category.

So, the problem of specific evil, the need for emancipation, a theory of general good and then coercive Utopia as a repository—perhaps *the* respository—of ideas of general good: this might be the conflict of interests that confronts us as we abandon both the folklore of modern architecture and the Popperian destruction of allied propositions; and it is a dilemma which seems to leave us only with the alternatives of Utopia and freedom—with freedom dependent upon Utopia and Utopia always acting to limit freedom.

In American terms this is a quandary which can often become the rule of law versus the will of the people—with 'law' or 'the people' idealized as the purpose of the occasion might seem to require. But, if this pair of opposites presumes an important willingness to argue and no great willingness to insist, it might also be transferable from the area of ostensible politics to the area of criticism in general. So there are no criteria which cannot be faulted, which are not in continuous fluctuation with their opposites. The flat becomes concave. It also becomes convex. The pursuit of an idea presumes its contradiction. The external world and the senses both equivocate; and criticism, however empirical it may sometimes profess to be, depends always upon an act of faith, upon an assumption ('this is a government of laws not men') of impossible realities but plausible abstractions. But, if the possible, the probable, and the plausibly abstract are always in a continuous condition of intersection, it is perhaps in some such area, where myth and reality interfecundate, that we should be willing to place all extreme fantasies both of Utopia and liberty.

The myth of Utopia and the reality of freedom! Alternatively: the reality of Utopia and the myth of freedom! However stated, what we have here are the intimately interwoven presumptions of both authority *and* liberty; and, if they are—both sets—necessary for survival, both of them the necessary components of discourse, then, if we profess any interest in emancipation but are not anxious to propose anarchy, perhaps it should only be said that *some* affirmation of a limited Utopia remains a psychological obligation. Utopia, in any developed form, in its post-enlightenment form, must surely be condemned as a monstrosity; but, while always a flagrant sociological or political nightmare, as a reference (present even in Popper), as a heuristic device, as an imperfect image of the good society, Utopia will persist—but should persist as possible social metaphor rather than probable social prescription.

## Notes

1 Thomas More, *Utopia*, Book II, Ch. II.

2 Plato, *Timaeus*, Bollingen series, 1944, p. 117.

3 James Leoni, *The Architecture of Leon Battista Alberti in Ten Books . . .* , London, 1735, Book VII, Ch. IV.

4 Isaac Ware, *The Four Books of Palladio's Architecture*, London 1738, Book IV, Preface.

5 Leoni, Book VII, Ch. III.

6 This is not entirely to discount the splendid Bramantesque piazza at Vigevano dating from the 1490s.

7 See Horst de la Croix, "Military Architecture and the Radial City Plan in Sixteenth Century Italy," *Art Bulletin*, Vol. XLII, no. 4, 1960.

8 Though this might seem to be a somewhat perfunctory handling of Saint-Simon, Fourier, Owen, *et al.*, one might still agree with Karl Mannheim that these were "dreaming their Utopias in the older intellectualist style" (Mannheim, *Ideology and Utopia*, 1st English ed., 1936; reprinted, New York, n.d., p. 245).

9 And one might again agree with Mannheim that "Where as in France, . . . the situation matured into a political attack the intellectualistic took on a rational form with decisively sharp contours. [But] where it was not possible to follow in this path, as in Germany, the Utopia was introverted and assumed a subjective tone." In Germany, Mannheim continues, "the road to progress was not sought in external deeds or revolutions, but exclusively in the inner constitution of man and its transformations." Mannheim, p. 220.

10 Mannheim, p. 192.

11 Sir Joshua Reynolds *Literary Works*, London, 1835, Vol. I, p. 333. From Discourse III delivered in 1770.

12 Carroll William Westfall, Review of Hermann Bauer, *Kunst und Utopie*, in *Journal of the Society of Architectural Historians*, Vol. XXVI, No. 2, 1967.

13 "A harmony of all the parts in whatsoever subject it appears, fitted together with such proportion and connection, that nothing could be added, diminished, or altered but for the worse": Alberti's definition of beauty (Leoni, Book VI, Ch. II) might also serve to illustrate the obvious predicament of Utopia with reference to both history and change.

14 Robin Marris, "Utopia and Conviction," *Granta*, Vol. LXIII, No. 1187, 1959.

15 See particularly the article, first published in the *Hibbert Journal* 1948, in the collection *Conjectures and Refutations*, New York and London, 1962. But the judgments which Popper here expresses are obviously to be found more extensively developed in his *The Logic of Scientific Discovery* (first published as *Logik der Forschung*, Vienna, 1934), London 1958; in *The Open Society and its Enemies*, London, 1945; and in *The Poverty of Historicism*, London, 1957. A valuable and appreciative criticism of Popper's centrality to the construction of any adequate contemporary critical theory is to be found in G. Radnitzky, *Contemporary Schools of Meta-Science*, Chicago, 1973.

16 That Popper could be overlooked by the contributors to a student magazine in 1959 perhaps should not be surprising; but that a similar failure should have characterized the contributors to vol. 94, no. 2, of the *Proceedings of the American Institute of Arts and Sciences* might arouse curiosity. However the issue *Utopia* of Daedalus, Spring 1965, appears nowhere to display a cognizance of his position.

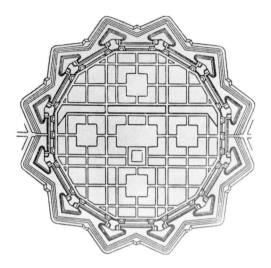

Plate 75   Plan for an ideal city. From Vincenzo Scamozzi, *L'Idea dell architettura universale*, Venice, 1615. This and the city shown in Plate 76 are neither Sforzinda nor Palma Nova. But as Sir Thomas More said of Utopian demonstrations, "They are indeed so alike that he that knows one knows them all."

Plate 76   Plan for an ideal city. From Buonaiuto Lorini, *Delle Fortificatione Libri Cinque*, Venice, 1592.

Plate 77   Francesco di Giorgio (?), *Perspective of a Square, c.* 1470.

Plate 78   Bramante, *Street Scene, c.* 1500-10 (?).

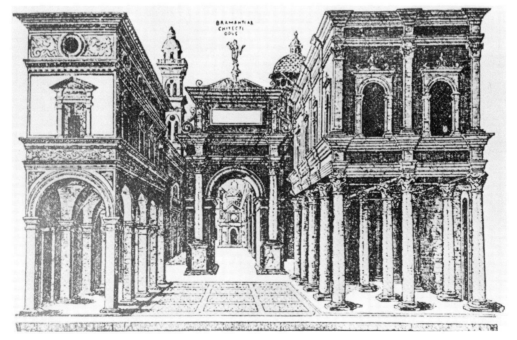

Plate 79  Project, La Saline de Chaux.
Claude-Nicolas Ledoux, 1775-79.

Plate 80  Project, Cenotaph for Newton.
Elevation and section. Etienne Louis
Boullée, 1784.

# VIEW OF THE COLLEGES FOR THE HAPPY COLONY

to be established in New Zealand by

The Workmen of Great Britain

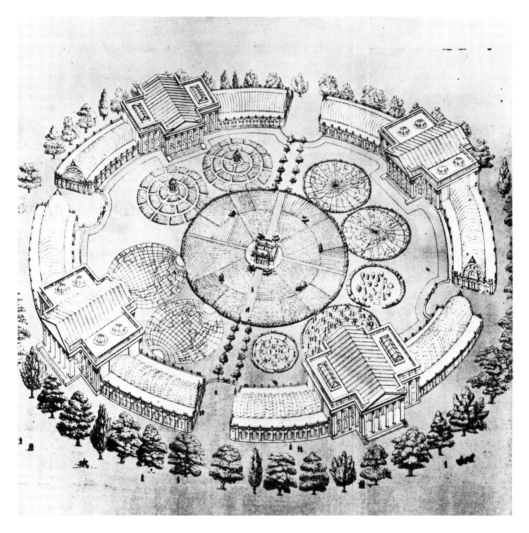

THE COLLEGES PLACED IN THE CENTRE OF THE TOWN, IN A CIRCLE OF FIFTY ACRES, SHEWING THE WORKSHOPS, BATHS, CONSERVATORIES, BOTANIC & HORTICULTURAL GARDENS
THE TERRESTIAL & CELESTIAL MAPS, LAID OUT ON THE GROUND, THE CIRCULAR GROVES, EMBODYING HISTORY, THE MUSES, MYTHOLOGY, THE MINIATURE FARM &c

Plate 81   The Happy Colony. From Robert
Pemberton, *The Happy Colony*, London,
1854.

Plate 82   Futurist study. Mario Chiattone, 1914.

Plate 83   Project, Plan Voisin. Le Corbusier, 1925.

# Picture Credits

Figure 1, J. Bostick. 2, Le Corbusier and P. Jeanneret, *Oeuvre Complète 1910-29*, Artemis, Zurich. 3, J. S. Ackerman, *The Architecture of Michaelangelo*, Zwemmer, London, 1961. 4, 5, P. Johnson, *Mies van der Rohe*, Museum of Modern Art, 1947. 7-9, H. R. Hitchcock, *In the Nature of Materials*, Duell, Sloan, & Pearce, New York, 1942. 10, Marcel Breuer & Associates. 11, Mies Archives, Museum of Modern Art. 12-15, *Oppositions 1*. 16, 17, Louis Kahn. 18-20, Gropius Archives, Busch-Reisinger Museum. 21, B. Hoesli. 22, Le Corbusier, *Towards a New Architecture*, tr. by F. Etchells, Architectural Press, London, 1948. 23, *Oeuvre 1952-57*. 24, *Oeuvre 1910-29*. 25, redrawn from *Oeuvre 1952-57*.

Plate 1, C. Rowe. 2, *Oeuvre 1929-34*. 3, Roberto Pane, *Andrea Palladio*, Einaudi, Turin, 1961. 4, G. Zorzi, Trieste. 5, 6, *Oeuvre 1910-29*. 7, redrawn from *Oeuvre 1910-29*. 8, G. Zorzi, *Le ville e i teatri di Andrea Palladio*, Neri Pozza, Vicenza, 1969. Photo Tapparo and Trentin. 9, *Le ville*. 10, Le Corbusier, *Le Corbusier et Pierre Jeanneret*, Morance, Paris, n.d. 11, *Andrea Palladio*. 12, *Oeuvre 1910-29*. 13, 14, C. Rowe. 15, 16, *Oeuvre 1957-65*. 17, *Towards a New Architecture*. 18, C. Rowe. 19, G. Zorzi, *Le opere pubbliche e i palazzi privati di Andrea Palladio*, Neri Pozza, Vicenza, 1965. 20, C. Rowe. 21, H. Kulka, *Adolph Loos*, Schroll, Munich, 1931. 22, Gropius Archives. 23, H. Bayer, W. Gropius, I. Gropius, *Bauhaus 1919-28*, Allen & Unwin, 1939. 24, Gropius Archives. 25, *Bauhaus 1919-28*. 26, *Architecture of Michaelangelo*. 27, *Oeuvre 1929-34*. 28, *New Vitruvius Britannicus*. 29, H. S. Goodhart-Rendel, *English Architecture since the Regency*, Constable, London, 1953. 30, Royal Commission on Historical Monuments, London. 31, 32, A. Downing and V. Scully, *The Architectural History of Providence, R. I.*, Harvard, Cambridge, Mass., 1952. Photos Mersevey. 33, R. Blomfield, *Richard Norman Shaw R.A.*, Batsford, London, 1940. 34, *English Architecture*. 35, *Richard Norman Shaw*. 36, A. Downing and V. Scully, *The Architectural Heritage of Newport, Rhode Island*, Potter, New York, 1967. 37, H. R. Hitchcock, "Frank Lloyd Wright and the Academic Tradition," Journal of the Warburg and Cortland Institutes, vol. 7, nos. 1, 2. 38, C. W. Condit, *The Rise of the Skyscraper*, Chicago, Chicago, 1952. 39, *Nature of Materials*. 40, Theodore Brown Rietveld. 41, S. Giedion, *Space, Time, and Architecture*, Harvard, Cambridge, Mass., 1954. Photo R. B. Tague. 42-46, *Nature of Materials*. 47, *Rise of the Skyscraper*. 48, 49, *Space, Time, and Architecture*. 50, *Mies van der Rohe*. 51, 52, Ezra Stoller photo, ©ESTO. 53, Fred Winchell photo. 54, Ezra Stoller photo, ©ESTO. 55, Roche, Dinkeloo Associates. 56, 57, Hedrich Blessing photos. Plans: Mies Archives, Museum of Modern Art. 58, Phillips Collection, Washington, D.C. 59, Douglas Cooper. 60, La Roche Collection, Kunstmuseum, Basle. 61, private collection. 62, Kunstmuseum, Bern. 63, 64, private collections. 65, Gropius Archives. 66, Catalogue, Picasso Exhibition, Museum of Modern Art, 1939. 67, Gropius Archives. 68, Hoesli, Zurich. 69, J. Bostick. 70-74, *Oeuvre Complète 1957-65*. 75-81, C. Rowe. 82, G. Veronesi, "Disegni di Mario Chiattone 1914-1917," *Comunita*, vol. 16 (March-April 1962). Original in Museo d'Architettura Moderna, Milan.